Paul Molitor
GOOD TIMING

The end of Molitor's Milwaukee era.

BUCK MILLER, SPORTS ILLUSTRATED

Paul Molitor

GOOD TIMING

A biography by STUART BROOMER

ECW PRESS

CANADIAN CATALOGUING IN PUBLICATION DATA

Broomer, Stuart
Paul Molitor : Good timing

Includes bibliographic references.
ISBN I-55022-207-4
I. Molitor, Paul. 2. Toronto Blue Jays (Baseball team) –
Biography. 3. Baseball players – Canada – Biography.
4. Baseball players – United States – Biography. I. Title.

GV865.M65B7 1994 796.357'092 C94-930593-6

Design and imaging by ECW Type & Art, Oakville, Ontario.
Printed by Data Reproductions, Rochester Hills, Michigan.

Distributed by General Distribution Services, Limited,
30 Lesmill Road, Don Mills, Ontario M3B 2T6,
(416) 445-3333, (800) 387-0172 (Canada), FAX (416) 445-5967.

Distributed to the trade in the United States exclusively by
InBook, 140 Commerce Street, P.O. Box 120261,
East Haven, Connecticut, U.S.A. 06512,
(203) 467-4257, FAX (203) 469-7697
Customer service: (800) 253-3605 or (800) 243-0138.

Published by ECW PRESS,
1980 Queen Street East,
Toronto, Ontario, Canada M4L IJ2.

TABLE OF CONTENTS

ACKNOWLEDGEMENTS

Thanks are due to some people who made this book possible: Jack David, for suggesting the book and providing helpful input along the way; Linda Murrell, for much of the archival research in Minneapolis-St. Paul and Milwaukee; Scott Mitchell, for detailed editing and many useful suggestions; my wife, Cherie, for reading and commenting on the manuscript as it developed; and our sons, Geoffrey and Stephen, for their joy in baseball.

ABOUT THE AUTHOR

A longtime baseball fan, Stuart Broomer writes regularly on music and the visual arts. He has taught English at several Ontario colleges and universities and is currently teaching at Centennial College in Toronto.

I

"The best-kept secret in baseball"

Only moments after Joe Carter hit a home run to end the 1993 World Series, Paul Molitor was named Most Valuable Player for his role in taking the Blue Jays to their second championship. It was the perfect award for Molitor, the crowning achievement of a long career. No other trophy could say as much about a brilliant ball player who was so committed to team achievement.

The single season that Molitor had spent with the Jays was a wonderful coming together of a team and a player that had spent almost the same length of time in the majors. The Toronto Blue Jays entered the American League East as an expansion franchise in 1977. Paul Molitor entered the American League East a year later, as a player for the Milwaukee Brewers. Success came suddenly for Molitor, more slowly for the Jays. But as the Jays built success upon success in the late '80s and early '90s, Molitor labored for a struggling franchise that seldom glimpsed the post-season. If circumstances finally intervened to take Paul Molitor out of Milwaukee's County Stadium and put him in Toronto's SkyDome, it was a chance earned by 15 years of effort in a franchise that could no longer afford the kind of team on which he could perform to his limits.

Paul Molitor — Minnesota Gopher.

In his 16 years in major league baseball, Paul Molitor has known most of the intense highs and lows the sport has to offer. Voted to the All-Star team in just his third season in the majors, he was prevented from playing by injuries. In his third and fourth years as a pro, he spent extended periods on the disabled list and flirted with cocaine use. He went to his first World Series in his fifth year in the majors. In 1984 he spent the year on the disabled list for a last-place team and suffered the ignominy of having his drug abuse revealed in a drug dealer's widely publicized trial. In 1987 he knew some of the terrors that come to those who chase legends, when he pursued Joe DiMaggio's record for hits in consecutive games.

The career of a Paul Molitor is measured in years and instants, seasons and nanoseconds. It is measured in months spent on the disabled list and the time it takes to bare-hand a bunt on the third base line and execute the throw to first. It is compounded of the durability that keeps a man playing season after season of pro baseball and the genius that rides in his synapses and reflexes. It unites the discipline of training camp and workouts and the freedom to throw oneself toward an elusive bag, to keep throwing oneself long after one has learned what the physical price of that determination can be.

Early in the season with the Toronto Blue Jays, facing the Yankees in Toronto's SkyDome, Molitor was on second when a ground ball was hit into the infield. With explosive speed, calculated pauses, and acute observation, he somehow managed to steal home. It wasn't just speed, but a brilliant feint that had allowed him to do it, his mind quicker than a defender's arm.

Similar things often happen when he is running the base paths. He has managed to steal home with a surprising frequency, and he has been judged by coaches to be the best base runner in the game. That doesn't come from just being faster than other players. Molitor is fast, but he's not as fast as he once was or as fast as some of his current teammates. It's something else again: it's the ability to calculate the reaction time of others, to gauge the complex intervals and possibilities alive in the field.

The same quickness is apparent every time Molitor goes to the plate. He seems always to be swinging late, to be swinging when the optimum instant for contact surely will have passed, when a foul tip or a strike is the only possibility. It is not an interval of judgement that is granted to even the "average" professional athlete, whose reaction time is never average, and it is likelier to appear in the driver of a Formula One car than in a baseball player.

Molitor's special gift of stretching time until it almost seems to have stopped is akin to the way Michael Jordan appears to hang suspended in midair, or the way the players of an opposing team seem to freeze in that instant when Wayne Gretzky pulls the puck around a goal post and puts it into the net. In that prolonged interval, Molitor's reflexes buy every available, microscopic particle of time for his judgement and his eyes, so that they can evaluate a pitch — weigh it, measure it, pace it, calculate its curve or spin — just a little longer. It is perhaps that extended interval of judgement, that concentrated synchronism of eyes, mind, and arms, that makes Paul Molitor just a little bit better at what he does than other hitters, and explains why he finished first in hits in the 1993 regular season, as he had done before in 1991. Molitor's knowledge of the physics of baseball allows him to be getting better at age 37, to be reaching new levels at a stage in his career when most have retired and those left have begun to wane.

Molitor is a magician with time in more ways than one. If he is among those few athletes who can seem to stop time, it is perhaps because he has had to. His career has been interrupted by injury with a terrible frequency. His seasons have often ended in surgery, and his off-seasons have been spent in rehabilitation. He has generated remarkable numbers for hits and runs and averages, but those numbers were sometimes lowered by the amount of time he spent languishing on the disabled list or playing while injured. His drive and his love of the game have kept him going, allowing him to surmount the serious, frequent, and persistent injuries, a long career out of the spotlight of a major market, and even a reputation for being a "fragile" player.

Paul Molitor's first major league manager called him "Mr. Clutch." In his first year in the pros, he acquired the nickname "The Igniter," later to become "The Ignitor" in a spelling mistake that enshrined his name at the same time that he objected to the error. The name captures the explosiveness of his play, that sudden element of surprise, whether at bat or on the bases, that is his signature. His last manager with the Brewers, Phil Garner, announced "He's baseball's secret." Almost a year later, as the Jays readied for the post-season, Toronto manager Cito Gaston called him "the best-kept secret in baseball." Bill James describes him as simply "a great player." The *Toronto Star*'s Rosie DiManno called him "Mr. Baseball." At the end of the 1993 American League Championship Series, one teammate, Ed Sprague, called him "the consummate ball player." Another teammate, Dave Stewart, a veteran of many post-seasons, called him "my favorite player."

How had a player like that managed to escape the limelight? There could be many reasons. That he played for 15 years on a small-market team, away from the glare of major media exposure, is the usual answer. He only appeared in post-season play once, in 1982, and when he did he was surrounded by older, more celebrated teammates in an ultimately losing cause.

But there are other reasons as well. As a Milwaukee Brewer, he was shuffled from one position to another. An excellent infielder, Molitor would, during his years with the Brewers, find service at shortstop, third, second, and first base, center, right and left field. There are only seven other players in the history of the game who have played over 50 games at each infield position. As good as he was as an infielder, Molitor would never be as good as he could be, only as good as time permitted to learn a new position. Unlike most major stars, it was hard to identify Molitor with a position. Increasingly in recent years, Molitor has been playing as designated hitter, but once a player settles into the DH role, as Molitor has, he isn't so much playing a position as representing an anomaly, a strange variation of the American League rule book. Molitor's injury-wracked career has seldom allowed him the totals he might have accumulated otherwise. There's also the question of power. A hitter who racks up home runs on a regular basis is immediately noticeable, whatever his home market, for the same reason that heavyweight boxers get the lion's share of publicity and money. Molitor hasn't stood out in this area.

Molitor's play is consistent, but what has made it special is its explosiveness. One reason his performance over the years has gone largely unnoticed outside of Milwaukee is that his best moments often seem like flukes: like stealing three bases in an inning, or hitting three homers in a game, or stealing home from second on an infield grounder, or getting five hits in a game in his first trip to the World Series. Those are the kinds of things a partisan fan might want to forget when they're happening to the home side, but they are the kinds of moments that have happened throughout Molitor's career. He has always been poised to bring off the unlikely, combining intuition, calculation, and reflexes in a way that is uniquely his own.

His potential highlight film would have played very differently if it belonged to another personality. Molitor is articulate and willing to talk at length to reporters, but one of his strongest traits is his modesty. He is the ultimate team player. He has seldom exhibited the kind of ego that one might expect from his feats. He never struts after a brilliant play, never rubs the noses of opposing players or fans in the particular genius of something he's just done. If he had, he'd be less well liked in baseball circles, and far better known to the larger baseball public.

2

From St. Paul to Minneapolis

Paul Molitor was born on August 22, 1956, in St. Paul, Minnesota. Richard and Kathy Molitor's family would eventually expand to eight children, six girls and two boys. It was a close family, and its very size would contribute to some of Molitor's qualities — his modesty and his devotion to team achievements.

As a boy, Paul Molitor revealed both remarkable athletic talent and a tendency to injury. At age eight he fell out of a tree and broke his arm. The injuries were always part of how he played, and Molitor's repeated injuries might have almost as much to do with the course of his career as his brilliance at baseball. A gifted athlete, his baseball prowess was already evident by the time his hometown Minnesota Twins went to the World Series in 1965. Paul was nine, but he had already been a devoted fan for four years. In St. Paul and Minneapolis television sets were wheeled into classrooms for the series. The Twins had great hitters in the '60s, like Harmon Killebrew and Tony Oliva. Killebrew had the most power, and Oliva had power and the most consistency. There was also the very quick shortstop Zoilo Versalles.

Molitor's talents were abundantly apparent when he entered Cretin High School in St. Paul. Paul's play had already benefited from John Hermes' excellent coaching in grade school. His coach with the Cretin Raiders, Bill Peterson, saw a student with very unusual abilities: "I first thought of Molitor as having the potential to become a professional when he was in the ninth grade."

"He was always an exceptional player," Peterson later recalled. "He had a very strong arm, which is interesting because he fell out of a tree when he was younger and hurt a muscle in his back, which affected his throwing. But when it healed, it came out stronger than it was."

With Peterson's teams, Molitor would frequently pitch, as well as playing shortstop and center field. Peterson coached Molitor both at Cretin High and on St. Paul's Attucks Brooks team in the American Legion league. The Legion teams competed against each other throughout the Midwest, and for the young Paul Molitor it was a chance to do some traveling and occasionally to compete with other students who were as talented as he was.

Peterson was delighted to have so gifted an athlete on his teams and worked hard to correct a critical flaw in Molitor's hitting. "On his swing, I could never get him to put his back foot in place. On the swing you're supposed to shift your weight and pivot on the ball of your back foot. But Paul never did that. He would lift his back foot on the swing and drag it."

Even in high school Molitor was plagued by frequent injuries, so that he was never, in Peterson's assessment, playing at full strength. In his final year of high school, Molitor missed the entire regular season with mononucleosis. "He wasn't supposed to practise," remembered Peterson, "but he begged and begged to hit. He must have had a month's worth of energy stored because he put on a hitting exhibition like I've never seen."

Molitor rejoined the Cretin Raiders for playoff games, and the team won the Central Catholic High School title. That sent them on to the State Independent League Tournament. In the final game of the tournament, Molitor went up to bat with the bases loaded in the fourth inning. Molitor didn't see Bill Peterson's take sign on a pitch, but he knew enough to expect it. "It was a bad pitch, really upstairs," Molitor told a reporter. "It was right about my chin and I couldn't pass it up. I hadn't had an extra-base hit in four games. It was a good thing I hit it out or it would have been my neck." Still recovering from the weakening effects of mononucleosis, the young shortstop had hit the bad pitch 380 feet. Bill Peterson could only comment, "How do you get mad at a guy for hitting a grand-slam home run?" The Raiders won the game by a score of 6–1 to repeat as state champions.

When the San Diego Padres drafted St. Paul's Dave Winfield in 1973, it created a new interest in the baseball that was being played in the north. Major league scouts began paying attention to the quality of players who were developing in Minnesota, and Molitor and Jack Morris were among the first to attract notice. Somehow the wintry confines of the northern state had, in a few short years, nurtured three players who would go on to merit consideration for Baseball's Hall of Fame. The short Minnesota baseball season seemed to be fueling a desire to excel. Clearly the talent was there, but there was also the coaching to nurture it. Winfield would go straight from college ball to the majors without passing through minor league baseball.

In his senior year of high school, Molitor's talent was sufficiently apparent to attract the notice of scouts from both colleges and major league teams. Creighton University and the University of Arizona were among the first to discuss the possibilities of an athletic scholarship. Reviews from the major leagues were mixed. Molitor was most disappointed in the lack of attention from the Minnesota Twins. In the assessment of his hometown franchise, Molitor was too small and would never have a career in major league baseball. A scout for the St. Louis Cardinals, Cobby Saatzer, saw things differently and recommended that the Cardinals offer Molitor a contract after picking him in the 25th round of the entry draft. Higher-ups in the Cardinals farm department, however, didn't share in Saatzer's enthusiasm. The team was only willing to authorize an offer of four thousand dollars, which Saatzer didn't think was enough to convince Molitor to sign.

Any interest that Molitor might have had in the Cardinals' offer ended a week later, when he was confronted with a clear choice between a trip to the minors and a university education. He went to the University of Minnesota at Minneapolis-St. Paul when he was offered a scholarship by Dick Siebert, long-time coach of the university's Minnesota Gophers. Siebert, known to his players as "Chief," had been at Minnesota since 1947 and was a gifted coach with an eye for talent. In Molitor he saw the best baserunning instincts of any player he'd ever encountered in amateur or professional baseball. Tom Mee, a fellow player with the '76 Gophers, later recalled Siebert saying several times that Molitor was without a doubt the best major league prospect he'd ever seen.

John Anderson, student manager of the Gophers in 1977 and later their coach, thought that "during tryouts Molitor just stood heads above everyone else, from the first day he walked on campus." Though Molitor was quiet, Siebert was quick to use him as an example for the rest of the team. Molitor was an aggressive player, always going after the ball, a player who would lead by example. He was selected as All-American in 1976 and was picked as co-captain of the Gophers for the 1977 season.

Apart from "natural" ability, Paul Molitor was an ardent student of baseball, both its history and its technique. An assistant coach with the Gophers, George Thomas, observed: "Just as you have advanced students come into college, Paul

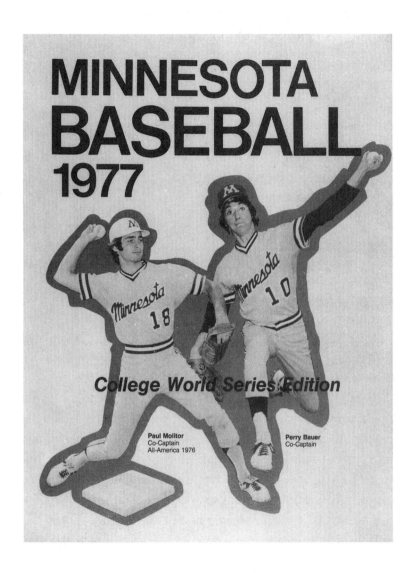

MINNESOTA
BASEBALL
1977

College World Series Edition

Paul Molitor
Co-Captain
All-America 1976

Perry Bauer
Co-Captain

COURTESY UNIVERSITY OF MINNESOTA ARCHIVES

was an advanced athlete coming onto our baseball team. You didn't have to work on fundamentals with him, but you could talk about theories."

Molitor's commitment to the team is evident in his memories of his play with the Gophers. It was the team that he recalled, not the string of records that he assembled in college ball. "We really tried to build team unity that year," he has recalled of 1977. "The year before we had a good team, but we didn't own up to our potential. I had a great year in '76, but we had a much better team in '77. Everyone worked hard and it showed in our success."

That team spirit was apparent when the Gophers voted for most valuable player, following their Big Ten win. When the votes were cast, student manager John Anderson received 22; Molitor received 1. The lone vote for Molitor had been cast by John Anderson. "John Anderson embodied what we had in mind that season," Molitor has explained. "He did everything except play. He was a groundskeeper, equipment man, assistant coach, and even a confidante for many of the players. He was very exceptional, so we decided he should get the award."

Molitor majored in education at university and planned on pursuing a career in coaching, but his first priority was getting a chance to play major league baseball. He spent the summer of 1976 playing with other major league prospects in Grand Junction, Colorado, on a team managed by Sam Suplizio, a scout for the California Angels. It was a chance to hit against better pitching than he faced in college ball, and a chance to impress Suplizio and other scouts from the majors. Interest in Molitor was definitely growing for the 1977 draft.

As Molitor prepared for the 1977 College World Series with his fellow Gophers, he learned that he had been drafted third overall by the Milwaukee Brewers, after the Chicago White Sox had taken Harold Baines and the Montreal Expos had taken Bill Gullickson. The Minnesota Twins, now anxious to draft him, had missed their chance. "It took me a little while to get down to the ground," he told a reporter after a Gopher practice. "There were a lot of local TV cameras there because some of my teammates were also drafted today." Molitor was already being self-effacing, deflecting the spotlight to the rest of his teammates in his own moment in the glare. Only one other Gopher, catcher Tom Jagiela, had been drafted up to that point. The cameras were for Molitor, the offensive sensation of college baseball that year. Molitor signed with the Brewers for $85,000, a significant sum for a rookie at the time.

Molitor didn't have to make claims for his ability. The stats would do it, and so would Dick Siebert. In his three seasons with the Gophers, Molitor had set five single-season records and seven college-career records. As a freshman, he had a .343 batting average, set a Minnesota record with six triples, and stole 23 bases. From then on his numbers had only gotten better. He ended his college baseball years with a career average of .350, 99 RBIS, and 52 stolen bases, despite missing time with a broken jaw suffered in a game. Dick Siebert declared, "I have made the statement before that I thought he had more ability than any player I have ever coached, and I've coached Dave Winfield, so that's a pretty tall order."

Molitor was already aware of Robin Yount's hold on the shortstop position with the Brewers, but he was prepared to be respectful and flexible. "I know that Mr. Yount is a tremendous shortstop. I've seen him play before. It wouldn't bother me if they moved me around. I've had more experience at second, but we'll have to wait and talk about that."

Years later, Molitor would still recall the first visit to Milwaukee's County Stadium. "The Brewers had just drafted me as an infielder, and they invited me to the park — really rolled out the red carpet for me," he would tell Richard Stoffer of *Sports Illustrated*. "I've still got a picture of myself sitting on the bench. My coat and tie are way too big. I'm totally geekish,

Gophers' publicity photos.

and I'm sitting in the dugout with Robin, who was in uniform. He may have been 21 or 22, but he'd already had something like four full seasons. I called him Mr. Yount, I remember that. And Sal Bando threw Robin an outfielder's glove and said, 'Well, I guess this will be your last year at shortstop, kid.' All I wanted was to get out of there."

"Mr. Yount," the seasoned professional, was less than a year older than Molitor. Drafted by Milwaukee in '73, a year before St. Louis drafted Molitor, Yount had gone straight to the majors in 1974.

At the end of the college season, a 20-year-old Paul Molitor went to Iowa to play with the Burlington Bees, Milwaukee's class-A farm team in the Midwest League. His manager was Denis Menke, who had just taken up his first managing position, two years after ending his own career as an infielder in the majors. Molitor had been a "pull, power hitter" in college, responsible for driving in runs with the Gophers. Menke was working at turning him into a contact hitter, developing his control, helping Molitor develop the skills that would lead to a long career in the majors.

Menke didn't expect to keep Molitor long. Other managers in the league could see it as well and kept warning Menke of his impending loss. Molitor was clearly the best player in the league. When he joined the Bees at the mid-point in their season, the team had a 28–42 record and was in last place. In his first professional game with the Bees, Molitor started what would become an 18-game hitting streak, and the team was on its way to first place. Menke was impressed by the way that Molitor would throw himself into the game. If Molitor was on second with two out, Menke knew that Molitor would find a way to get home. It was the kind of driven running and brilliant timing that Molitor would display later in the majors.

Menke got to keep Molitor longer than he might have, though, because the Bees were winning. Molitor was guaranteed a place in triple A after three weeks with the single-A team, but when the time came for his promotion he asked to stay in single A to help the team win the championship. He did, driving the Bees to the Midwest title and winning the league batting title with a .348 average. Molitor had spent his entire minor league career, a mere 64 games, in single A ball.

When Molitor's old coaches recall him as a young man, they invariably remember the most gifted ball player they had ever had the good fortune to meet. When Paul Molitor reminisces about those years, it is not the individual records he recalls but the team accomplishments. Profoundly modest, Molitor has always sought team victories. It is that passion to become one with a group, united in the moment of victory, more than the spotlight, that has driven his career. Whatever his gifts, he has always tried his hardest, and it is that unceasing effort that links him not with superstars, but with the journeymen of the sports world. It is what would make him so popular in the work-driven world of Milwaukee sports.

PAUL MOLITOR:
MILWAUKEE BREWER

"You've got a great swing, rookie — you can make it big."

Thurman Munson

3

The Rookie Year

In his early years with the Brewers, Molitor could feel part of a great organization, one that was clearly on the rise. At the end of 1969, Bud Selig had acquired a lackluster expansion franchise that had lasted only a single season as the Seattle Pilots. He was bringing major league baseball back to Milwaukee just four years after the Braves had migrated to Atlanta. It would take the next decade to bring them to contention.

The Brewers entered the majors in the American League West in 1970 and tied with Kansas City for fourth place. In 1971 they finished sixth of six in the division. In 1972 they moved to the American League East and again finished sixth, managing to be the worst team in two different divisions in consecutive seasons. For the next three seasons, 1973–1975, they managed to finish fifth. In 1976, they slipped back into sixth place, 32 games behind the division-leading Yankees. In 1977, they were again in sixth place, 33 games back of the Yankees. They were saved from the cellar only by the expansion entry of the Toronto Blue Jays who, in their first season, managed to be 12 games back of the Brewers. In 1978, Molitor's first season with the team, the Brewers' fortunes would take a dramatic turn for the better. They had a new general manager in Harry Dalton, a new manager in George Bamberger, and they were boosting their already potent hitting with Larry Hisle and Ben Oglivie.

In the winter of 1977–78, still in St. Paul, Molitor practised hitting in the University of Minnesota field house with Hisle, a veteran who was going to the Brewers from the Minnesota Twins as DH and outfielder. It was a special time for Molitor, practising with a man who had been a star with his hometown team since 1973. It was a chance to refine his hitting skills, and, as usual, he made the most of the opportunity. "I learned by watching him," Molitor would say a year later. He was working on the skills he had been acquiring with Denis Menke, emphasizing contact, stance, and field control, getting further away from the slugging approach. Working out with Hisle, refining his game, he was getting a sense of just how much power was involved in that approach in the majors.

At the Brewers' spring training camp in Chandler, Arizona, Molitor was impressive. George Bamberger was excited about the young shortstop's skills. "Has he got good actions! I like everything about that kid. He swings the bat good. He can run."

There was some uncertainty as to just how Molitor would fit into the Brewers' plans, however. They had plenty of good infielders: Cecil Cooper was at first base, Don Money and Lenn Sakata were platooning at second base, Robin Yount was at shortstop, and Sal Bando, veteran of the Oakland Athletics' World Series teams, was the regular third baseman, with Jim Gantner as a backup. Having too much talent was a new problem for the Brewers, and Bamberger was concerned with Molitor's development. "You need backup men, too, but naturally we want to do what's best for him. He should be playing every day." With the Brewers' infield, that would likely mean a trip to the minors.

But the Brewers had other immediate concerns. Robin Yount hadn't come to terms on a new contract, and there was

Katherine Molitor and poster of son Paul.

MARK MORSON, ST. PAUL PIONEER PRESS

a possibility that he would have to be traded. There was a chance the Brewers would need a regular shortstop.

At the end of spring training the Brewers had decided to send Molitor to Spokane, their triple-A franchise in the Pacific League. Just as the van was about to leave training camp, though, Molitor was called back to the clubhouse. Robin Yount had injured his foot and his contract was still unsigned. Molitor would at least be starting the season in the majors, at shortstop with the Brewers when the 1978 season began.

A GOOD START

In the opening home stand against the Orioles, the Brewers put on an extraordinary display of hitting for fans accustomed to the pain of lackluster expansion-team baseball. In the first game of the season, Molitor had only a single hit, but a grand-slam homer by Sixto Lezcano led the Brewers to an 11-run victory in front of 48,000 fans. Only 6,400 fans braved the cold the next day, but they got to witness an even more remarkable performance. Milwaukee pitcher Moose Haas gave up three runs to the Orioles in the top of the first inning. Molitor singled as the Brewers' first at bat, eventually getting home on singles by Don Money and Cecil Cooper. Larry Hisle hit a three-run homer, and Ben Oglivie singled to retire Dennis Martinez, the Orioles' starter. His replacement, Joe Kerrigan, walked two batters to load the bases before surrendering a grand-slam homer to Gorman Thomas. The Brewers ended the first inning with an 8–3 lead.

The Orioles' offense was through for the day, but the Brewers kept going, particularly Molitor. The Brewers would score eight more runs, and Molitor would be responsible for five of them, hitting a three-run homer in the fourth inning, then knocking in two more runs in the fifth with a single. The final score was 16–3.

Two games into the season and it looked like something had changed in the fortunes of the Brewers. The next day, a Sunday with gale-force winds blowing, found 18,000 fans in County Stadium to see what Bamberger and the Brewers could do. In the fourth inning, Larry Hisle drove in two runs with a bases-loaded single. A walk followed to load the bases again. Then, in defiance of the wind, Cecil Cooper drove a home run over the right-field fence. It was the third bases-loaded homer in as many games, a feat that had never been accomplished before in the American League, and hadn't happened in the National League since Pittsburgh had managed it in 1925, over 50 years before.

Molitor wasn't just in the majors. When the weekend series ended, the Brewers had scored 40 runs in three games, loading the bases 10 times. He was part of an incredible hitting machine, not just being there but making an important contribution.

On a team loaded with big hitters, Molitor was finding ways to get on base. In the second inning of the third game, with two men on base and two out, Molitor caught the third baseman playing well back of the base. He placed a perfect bunt down the third base line, managed to scurry to first, and got another runner home. Bamberger was ready to guarantee "that nine out of ten guys wouldn't have thought of it. He's a heads-up guy." Not knowing how long he'd be with the club, Molitor was making the most of every chance that he got. On another at bat that night, Molitor took a full swing, only to have the ball dribble down the third base line. He ran it out to first while the third baseman waited for the ball to wander into foul territory. It never did, instead managing to roll until it hit the bag. Molitor's legs and luck had given him another base hit.

Bamberger was delighted, telling reporters, "That kid is fantastic, boys. He is a fantastic kid. I have never seen a kid in my life like him." Molitor ended his first weekend in the majors with seven hits in 16 at bats, seven RBIs, and a home run. With the season three days old, he looked like a shoo-in for Rookie of the Year honors.

A few days later, Yount came to terms with the Brewers, and Molitor moved to second, where he was usually alternated with Jim Gantner. By the time Molitor finished a four-hit game in Toronto in mid-June, he had a batting average of .332.

In Cleveland, a few days later, Molitor sat out the first game of a doubleheader, a game in which the Brewers were shut out, ending a 10-game winning streak. Molitor entered the second game ready to run. He had already stolen two bases during the game when he went up to bat in the top of the ninth. He singled to score Jim Gantner, giving the Brewers a 3–1 lead. On the throw home to catch Gantner, Molitor headed for second and made a headfirst slide to beat the throw from home plate. When Robin Yount hit a fly to right field, Molitor got to third. He watched the first pitch, a ball, to Gorman Thomas and told the third base coach, Buck Rodgers, he was going to steal home. Rodgers laughed. He didn't think Molitor was serious, but said, "Okay. Just don't try it with two strikes." Molitor was scrutinizing the Indians' Dan Spillner with special care. Spillner had a slow windup, and he hadn't been looking over at Molitor at third. The Indians' third baseman, Buddy Bell, was playing well back of the base, making it hard for Spillner to pick Molitor off. When Thomas fouled off the second pitch, Molitor decided to steal on the next throw, taking a long lead off third. Spillner didn't notice him until he was almost through with his windup. Molitor made it home easily. He was halfway past the plate by the time catcher Bo Diaz tagged him. An exuberant Molitor claimed he "even slowed down to give the ball a chance to go by Gorman."

Bamberger was already calling Molitor "Mr. Clutch." After the steal, the manager admitted that the play surprised him.

*Rookie Paul Molitor signing autographs
at a junior all-star game in Milwaukee.*

CRAIG BORCK, ST. PAUL PIONEER PRESS

"Molitor has fantastic instincts on the bases. I'm really not a believer in stealing home, I'll tell you the truth. You only make it 20 percent of the time. But if you feel you have a good chance, go ahead. We let the kid run any time he feels he can make it, but I was as surprised as the pitcher." Buddy Bell was impressed too. The Indians' third baseman told Molitor that he was the best young player that Bell had seen come into the majors while he'd been playing.

In only a few short months, without time in AAA, Molitor had raised the brilliant timing that he'd shown in college ball to the major league level, managing to compute all the variables of windup, pitch, and distances in order to calculate his chances. In the years to come, the Brewers' managers would leave Molitor's decisions to steal, and how far to steal, up to him.

"Every day is a new thrill. I can't believe it," Molitor enthused to a reporter. For Molitor, with his deep respect for the game and its traditions, Fenway Park and Yankee Stadium were "hallowed ground." He had read about them since he was a little boy, and now he had a chance to play in them. Before his first game in Yankee Stadium, he walked out alone to centerfield to look at the stadium's statues, feeling a chill run through his body.

With his talent and enthusiasm, Molitor was welcomed into the league by many of the veterans he played against. When he played his first games against the Yankees, their veteran catcher, Thurman Munson, encouraged him when he came up to bat. "You've got a great swing, rookie — you can make it big," Munson told him. Molitor appreciated the boost to his morale. He and Munson became close friends through contacts in the Christian Athletes group, and Molitor was deeply saddened when Munson died just a year later in a plane crash. Munson's generosity of spirit would make him one of Molitor's role models.

Though he would sometimes shine, the promise of that first

stunning weekend wasn't to be immediately fulfilled. The consistently good play in the first half of the season gradually deteriorated. Bamberger and Molitor had different explanations for the problem. Bamberger thought Molitor was tired, not used to playing every day and to the travel schedule of the majors. Molitor knew that was part of it, but the alternating, too, was having an effect on his game. Breaking out of a batting slump in August, Molitor said, "I wasn't playing every day, and when I was playing, I was putting too much pressure on myself." The alternating led to a hitting slump, and the slump led to benching.

He was anxious about his place with the Brewers, and sometimes his insecurity would assert itself as brash over-confidence. Late in September, Molitor had a chance to play in two games in a row. He declared to a reporter, "I played two, and we won two." When given the opportunity, he would work through his slumps.

Though used sporadically at some points in the season, Molitor had been impressive. Despite being alternated at second and the brief benching during August, Molitor managed to play in 125 games in 1978. Bamberger didn't plan on using him in the stretch run, but Molitor's play almost demanded that he be brought back into the lineup. He ended the year with a batting average of .273 and a remarkable 30 stolen bases. Although his chances of winning the American League's official Rookie of the Year award had flagged as his batting average collapsed — he had hit just .158 during August and September — he was nonetheless picked as Rookie of the Year by *Sporting News*.

A REMARKABLE RISE

For the Brewers, 1978 was an unparalleled success. It was the season that saw them rise from the doldrums of expansion to become a team that could legitimately contend against the best in the American League East. While they could hardly live up to the promise of that incredible opening home stand, in their first season over .500 they were playing more than respectable baseball. Total wins went from 67 to 93. The winning percentage went from .414 to .574.

They were doing it with pure offensive baseball. While the team ERA was much improved, dropping from 4.32 to 3.65, the increase in runs was even more significant. In 1977, the Brewers had scored 639 runs. In 1978, they crossed the plate 804 times to lead the majors in runs. While that legendary Yankee team of the late '70s had again won 100 games, the last a stunning one-game playoff against Boston to decide the division, Milwaukee was 26 games closer to the front-runner.

Paul Molitor was in the right place at the right time, playing for a winning team that hadn't won before. Milwaukee in the late '70s and early '80s was a perfect environment in which to study the mechanics of hitting. The Brewers had both power hitters and contact hitters, and Molitor could learn from both.

The lineup included several men who could compete to lead the American League in home runs. The veteran Larry Hisle, coming to the Brewers at the same time as Molitor, had led the league in RBIs as a member of the Twins in 1977. At the end of the '78 season, Hisle was tied for second in the American League in homers, was second in slugging percentage, and third in RBIs. Sal Bando, a veteran of Oakland's three World Series wins, had come to the Brewers for the 1977 season. A natural leader with a tremendous drive to win, Bando had been second in the league in slugging average in 1973, in RBIs in 1974, and in home runs in 1976. Gorman Thomas, a Brewer since 1973, would lead the American League in homers in 1979 and tie for first place in 1982 with Reggie Jackson. Ben Oglivie, who also went to the Brewers in '78, would tie Jackson for first place in homers in 1980. That year, Thomas was next on the list. No other team in baseball enjoyed that kind of concentrated power.

The Brewers didn't just have power. Cecil Cooper and Robin Yount had two of the most consistent bats in baseball. Coming to the Brewers in 1977, Cooper would lead the league in RBIS in 1980 and tie for first place in 1983. In 1980, Cooper's .352 batting average and 219 hits would be second in the league in each category.

Robin Yount, though, was becoming the Brewers' most distinguished player, with consistent clutch hitting and brilliant fielding. Just 18 when he joined the Brewers for the 1974 season, he had matured in front of Milwaukee fans into the team's most important member, both defensively and offensively.

Although Yount might have the shortstop position sewn up, Molitor's offensive skills were a perfect fit for the team. He could get on base, and once on base he could use his speed to capitalize on the team's power hitters. Above all, a player with the baserunning skills of a Paul Molitor doesn't just add to the totals — he rattles an opposing pitcher. As often as not, a pitcher facing Yount or Cooper, Thomas or Oglivie, had to be aware of the action behind him, and the potential runs already on base. Molitor brought to the Brewers a baserunning talent that was apparent nowhere else in the lineup. Whether on base or at the plate, he had a knack for bringing off the unlikely.

4

Getting Established

Molitor went to spring training in 1979 without a contract. Negotiations had begun very late, with the Brewers not offering a contract until after the new year. The Brewers were offering a two-year pact, but Molitor and his agent, Ron Simon, wanted only a one-year contract. Molitor was confident he was going to have a good year and it would push up his value after the 1979 season. The process of negotiating was a new complexity for Molitor, and he had mixed feelings about it. The need for strategy and his own youthful enthusiasm didn't coexist easily. Both sides were stretching out the discussions. If the Brewers seemed to be treating the signing as an afterthought, Simon's strategy was to get down to the last two players to sign. That way, he and Molitor would see what other second-year players in the league were getting, and it would push up the Brewers' desire to get Molitor under contract.

At the same time, Molitor was concerned about giving the impression of holding out. "The fact that you're the last one to sign was hanging over my head. People kind of notice that and you don't want to get a bad name." The signing was a tremendous relief to him. The day of the signing he would tell some other players he was going to hit a homer in that day's exhibition game to make the contract worthwhile. He wanted to let the Brewers' general manager, Harry Dalton, know he was making a good deal. Molitor managed to get the homer. "There never was any doubt but that I would play here," he told a reporter after signing a one-year deal. "I wasn't going to walk out — not when I have a good thing going and working for a hell of a general manager." It was hard to negotiate with enthusiasm like that.

In the season to come, the Brewers and Paul Molitor got better, attracting growing attention throughout the American League. The big bats were even more noticeable than they'd been a year before, and throughout the season they stayed in pursuit of the Orioles. In just his second season, there was already talk about Molitor going to the All-Star team. White Sox vice-president Roland Hemond was among those who were impressed. When Molitor managed to score against the White Sox from second on an infield out, Hemond thought Molitor should already be getting national recognition.

The Brewers ended the year in second place with 95 wins and a winning percentage of .590, just behind an Oriole team that would go to the World Series. Playing 140 games, Molitor had a batting average of .322. After the regular season, still anxious to play, he joined a group of other American major-leaguers for a series of exhibition games in Japan.

A PULLED MUSCLE AND A BAD HABIT

The 1980 season started well for Molitor, with the young second baseman beginning to play at his potential. He was quickly pulling away from other hitters in the league, and by June 5th he had a league-leading average of .358. He was learning to be more selective about the pitches he swung at. "The more bad pitches you lay off of, the more you're able to keep your average up," he told a reporter. His skill at bunting was changing the way third basemen would play him, creating holes for him to hit through. More and more, he was setting the pace for the team. He and Yount were rapidly becoming the best leadoff and second hitter combination in baseball.

Then, on June 6, Molitor pulled a muscle in his rib cage. It would be his first trip to the disabled list, and it would be one filled with frustration. The injury didn't show signs of improving in the first few weeks. Meanwhile, the voting was going on for the All-Star Game, and Molitor, on the disabled list, was watching his vote mount and his team descend.

By the time the final count was in, Molitor had easily won the voting for second baseman. He had received 2,454,941 votes, 850,000 more than the second-place finisher. It was the most tangible recognition he'd received in his brief career, and he was pleased, but he was also conscious of how some of his teammates had fared. Robin Yount and Cecil Cooper were each in second place at shortstop and first base. "I have mixed emotions about it," Molitor confessed. "To be in the All-Star Game after just three years in the league is something you've always dreamed of. And you never know when you'll have another chance. But then I hear Bucky Dent [of the Yankees] beats out Robin. It's only because he's from the big-market city. It doesn't seem right. And Cecil is probably having a little better year than [the Angels'] Rod Carew."

By the time of the All-Star Game, Molitor's rib-cage injury was still bothering him and he was unable to play, but he went to Los Angeles as a spectator. He found that it hurt to watch other people swing, never mind trying it himself. A chance at a national audience had eluded him, but the frustration of the injury was worse. During the regular season, Molitor was watching games in which the Brewers were being shut out, losing to teams that managed a run. Watching from the stands, he would ask, "How long can we wait? How long can we wait?"

By the time he returned to the lineup, in mid-July, he had missed 40 games with the muscle pull. Out of shape from the long layoff, he was unable to return to his earlier hitting form, and his average for the year started to fall. He was making errors at second he wouldn't have made before. He was frustrated with his own play, and he was frustrated with the play of the Brewers. Usually reticent to speak negatively about the team, Molitor began venting his frustrations. When the Yankees pulled 13 games ahead of the Brewers, he questioned the work ethic of some of his teammates: "I think we've been a little lackadaisical at times. Possibly we're not giving the effort all the time . . . like running out ground balls. We have times when maybe some people aren't doing those things. I do know the Yankees know how to win. I don't know if we do. You can see it in the way they carry themselves."

When George Bamberger, who had been suffering from a heart condition, retired as manager of the Brewers in early September, Molitor particularly felt the loss. Bamberger had come to the team in the same season Molitor had arrived, and Bamberger, more than anyone else, had helped make the Brewers winners. The team couldn't rise to a victory on Bamberger's last day on the job, but Molitor certainly tried. He had four hits in five at bats, but couldn't find a way to score. It was disheartening. By season's end, Molitor's batting average had fallen to .304, and the Brewers, so close at the beginning, were 17 games back of the Yankees.

During the period of forced inactivity, Molitor, depressed, had begun to experiment with cocaine. It was hardly unusual at the time. Cocaine developed a tremendous popularity during the '70s, and one of the places it was popular was professional sports. Many major league teams, including the Brewers, had a small clique of regular users. The habit seemed harmless then, though time would show the ill effects on many lives and careers. By 1980, Molitor had grown used to

PAUL L. MOLITOR
Gophers
1975-1977
Shortstop

PAUL L. MOLITOR
Milwaukee Brewers 1983
Third Base

Playing baseball at Cretin High School, at the U of M and with the Milwaukee Brewers, I've had more than my share of injuries. I know the importance of proper diagnosis and treatment. Athletes of all ages, from rank amateurs to the pros also need a place where their physical abilities can be assessed so that the likelihood of injury can be lessened. That's why I'm supporting the University of Minnesota Sports Medicine Institute. I hope you'll join me by making your contribution or pledge, too.

Paul L. Molitor

the kind of attention and involvement his career entailed. Already emerging as a star on the team, he enjoyed the rounds of media appearances in Milwaukee, and was sought after for interviews, while his teammates' respect had already made him the Brewers' representative to the Major League Baseball Players Association. The inactivity that came with the rib-cage injury left him prey to frustration and depression, and the drug involvement was the result. Molitor's girlfriend was threatening to leave him if he couldn't stop. Eventually, during the 1981 season, he realized the potential cost both to his personal relationships and to his career. He managed to quit.

There's nothing positive about drug abuse. Molitor would later spend a great deal of time counseling young people not to make the same mistake. As he knew, it was very easy to slip into drug use. The same strengths of character and purpose that allowed Molitor to overcome his drug use would become increasingly apparent in his play.

AN INTERRUPTED SEASON

At the end of the 1980 season, Buck Rodgers took over as manager of the Brewers. One of the first decisions he made at spring training in 1981 was that Paul Molitor should play center field. The move would have immediate consequences. Molitor would be more concerned with learning the fine points of a new position than with concentrating on offense, while Gorman Thomas, irked at being shifted from center to right, would promptly stop speaking to Molitor.

The new position immediately took its toll on Molitor's hitting. His mechanics were off. He wasn't keeping his shoulder tucked in, and he was hitting a lot of weak ground balls. He had gone 0 for 22, his longest hitless streak in the majors, and had an average of .171 when the Brewers faced the Blue Jays in Toronto on April 21. That night he hit a double.

There must have been something about the cold that appealed to Molitor's Minnesota roots. The next night, in freezing temperatures, he found his form again, going 3 for 4 and managing to hit a grand-slam homer, the first time he'd done it in the major leagues. Before the game was over, though, he suffered a pulled groin muscle that would take him out of the lineup for a couple of games.

Then, on May 3, the Brewers faced the California Angels at Anaheim. In the first play of the game, Molitor tried to push a ground ball to a double. Lunging with his left foot, he landed on the backside of the bag, twisting his ankle. He took a few steps, then fell to the ground, clutching his left ankle, writhing in pain. Early diagnosis indicated a severe sprain. The Brewers expected to lose him for three to four weeks, but the injury was more serious than it first appeared. Molitor had torn ligaments and would require surgery. He would be out of the game for three months.

The ankle surgery was Molitor's personal interruption for the 1981 season. A players' strike would interrupt baseball for everyone else. Molitor would play in only 64 games that year, but the Brewers would play just 109. When the strike was resolved, the season was treated as two mini-seasons, with the leading teams from both halves meeting in a five-game playoff series to decide each division. In the AL East, the Yankees had won the first half. In the second half of the season, the Brewers found themselves in a race for first place with the Detroit Tigers.

Molitor finally returned to the lineup on August 12, but it took him a while to get his conditioning up. Buck Rodgers started him back as designated hitter and had him batting eighth in the lineup. Later in the month he would be out again with a groin pull.

The season all came down to a series in County Stadium against the Tigers, who needed to win two of three games to take over first place. The first Tiger batter, Alan Trammell, hit down the third base line. Molitor, playing right field for only the second time in his career, ran to make the catch, only to drop the ball. He was credited with an error, but the ball was ruled foul. Molitor had never dropped a pop-up or a fly ball in the majors until that moment. Trammell then hit a line drive to right-center. Molitor ran and dived and managed to make a brilliant catch. For Molitor it would later seem ironic. They were the only two plays he was called on to make in the game, and he'd handled them as badly and as well as anyone could. Luck held, and the Brewers were able to beat the Tigers both that day and the next to clinch the season's second half. The Brewers were making their first trip to the post-season, however unusual the circumstances.

Excitement ran high in Milwaukee for the series against the Yankees. The Brewers were playing in a territory that was new to them, facing Reggie Jackson, Dave Winfield, and the Yankees' pitching staff in the kind of games that really counted. That pitching was more than they had counted on. In the first two games, played in Milwaukee, the Yankees took a quick two game lead, winning 5–3 in the first and shutting out the Brewers 3–0 in the second.

When the games moved to New York, the Brewers clawed their way back into the series. In the third game, the Brewers played before a crowd of 56,411 who clearly thought Milwaukee shouldn't have bothered coming. It was New York. In the seventh inning a fan came out of the stands to attack the third base umpire. Somehow the Brewers found the incident invigorating. In the eighth inning, Molitor hit a fly ball to left field that looked like it might go out. It went into the stands, but Dave Winfield wouldn't let that deter him. Winfield climbed the ten-foot fence and went into the crowd to recover the ball as Molitor was running full out. Winfield didn't come up with the ball, and Molitor was passing third and heading for home when he realized he could enjoy the homer. It would prove to be the winning run. The Brewers were still alive.

The next day, in a game of tight pitching, the Brewers got another win, thereby managing to get what they had wanted when they came to New York: they had turned it into a one-game series. The only thing they couldn't deal with was another aspect of New York craziness. After the second loss, George Steinbrenner had a shouting match with Yankee catcher Rick Cerone in the clubhouse. Now the Yankees were determined to win in spite of their owner. A year earlier, Molitor had said, "The Yankees know how to win." The Yankees' fund of post-season experience would allow them to turn their game up a notch when it mattered, and Reggie Jackson was at the core of their determination. "If I'm not going to wear this uniform next year, I don't want to go out losing three in a row," he said. Cerone and Jackson would both hit home runs in a 7–3 Yankee win.

After the season, Molitor and Ron Simon were pressing for a long-term contract, but now it was the team's turn to be reluctant. The injuries were making the Brewers' organization look long and hard at Molitor's potential for the future. Eventually, he was signed to another one-year contract.

5

A Single-Minded Focus

The Brewers started 1982 knowing that they could compete. The 1981 season had shown them that. Paul Molitor started the new season with a healthy body, a renewed commitment to winning, and another new position. After two years at second base and a year moving around the outfield, he was now to become the regular third baseman. Molitor's sense of humor barely veiled some resentment of Buck Rodgers' plans: "Last year they told me I was the center fielder of the future. I'm going to start working on my slider. If something happens to Rollie Fingers, I might be the relief pitcher of the future."

The '82 Brewers were still a team devoted to hitting. While their pitching was sometimes inconsistent, they had the most potent offense in the American League. These two factors conspired to create very high scoring games. As often as not, though, especially early in the season, the points went to the other team.

On May 12, the Brewers faced the Royals in Kansas City, having lost the first two games in the series. The first game had been close, a 3–2 loss going to closer Rollie Fingers when he permitted a ninth-inning home run. The second game was humiliating, with the Royals running up a score of 17 to 3.

Molitor's response the next day was to push his own game

up a notch, coming back from the defeat to perform one of the outstanding offensive feats of his career. By game's end, he had managed three solo home runs — two off starter Dennis Leonard and one off reliever Dan Quisenberry — and an RBI single.

It was a performance that impressed George Brett. After the game, the Royals' third baseman remarked to another player in the dressing room, "Do you know if Molitor had a game like that every day, he'd hit over 500 home runs in a year? Imagine that!" Brett could afford to be impressed. In the visitors' clubhouse, Paul Molitor was just another member of a losing team. Even though he had just managed to hit one more home run in a single game than he had managed to hit in the strike-and-injury-shortened season of 1981, he couldn't find reason to celebrate. The Royals had beaten the Brewers once more, by a score of 9 to 7. It was the Royals' fifth victory in six meetings between the two clubs.

"Personally, it's satisfying having a good night, but you still want to come out of here and win at least one of these games. Losing the game kind of makes my night a little meaningless," Molitor remarked after the game. His thoughts were already on the future: "We've got to put this series behind us and try to salvage the road trip. You don't want this thing to start snowballing. We've got to go out and get that first one tomorrow, pick up where we left off when we came in here."

The next night, at Comiskey Park in Chicago, Tony LaRussa's White Sox beat the Brewers 13–2. The Brewers had now allowed 39 runs in 24 innings. They'd responded with 12 runs in 27. The scores were bearing out an old baseball truism: good pitching beats good batting. Despite the Brewers' lineup of heavy hitters, opposition pitchers often prevailed in the first two months of 1982, while the Brewers' own pitching, the best the team had ever enjoyed, was seldom good enough to carry them through.

Three weeks later, on June 2, Buck Rodgers was fired and Harvey Kuenn took over managing duties. The Brewers were in fifth place in the American League East, a game under .500. The change was felt immediately. Kuenn was a masterful handler of ball players' personalities, with an unerring sense of when to rein in a player and when to give one some room. By the time of the All-Star break, six weeks later, the team, inspired by Kuenn's direction, had won 25 games and lost 11. With the Brewers' bats invigorated, the team quickly became known as "Harvey's Wallbangers."

Recalling the frustration of 1981 and the loss to the Yankees in the division playoff, the Brewers had a single-minded focus on going to the World Series. When they moved into first place in the American League East just before the All-Star break, Gorman Thomas was already leading the league with 22 homers, but the veteran was now concentrating on team goals: "I've said a lot of times that personal goals don't really mean a lot until the end of the season. I still think that way. The most important thing is to get into the World Series. I want to win the World Series more than anything. That would be the ultimate." The more time that Molitor spent around veterans like Thomas and Cecil Cooper, the more the post-season would come to seem the only thing that really mattered in baseball. It was something even Molitor and Thomas could agree on.

Defense would be a source of some frustration for Molitor. At the end of the regular season, he would lead the American League in two stats for third basemen: errors and double plays. Both figures would say much about his fielding. The 29 errors were something he'd hear too much about. He was getting criticisms for being "all hit and no field." There was talk that he was "a good leadoff man, but can his teammates cover for him defensively?" Molitor felt the reputation was contributing to his error total, because if there was any doubt on a close play, the official would simply charge him with an error.

The stats for double plays were just as revealing. He simply played third base the way he played baseball — full out — and if that meant being charged with errors on a play that another third baseman might not have tried, so be it. The successful double plays were just as important as the errors, showing how the quickness in Molitor's running game could come into play when he was in the infield.

Through it all, Molitor was managing to stay healthy. On June 18, he was hit in the head by a ball pitched by Detroit's Milt Wilcox. It was a frightening moment when he went down, but he got right back up.

At the end of August, the Brewers acquired Don Sutton from the Houston Astros. He was the kind of pitcher they were going to need, a pitcher with post-season experience who had led the National League in 1980 with an ERA of 2.21. With Sutton added to starters Pete Vuckovich, Moose Haas, and Mike Caldwell, and reliever Rollie Fingers, the Brewers were finally balancing the offense with more quality on the mound.

The regular season ended dramatically. Three games up on the Orioles, the Brewers were facing them in a four-game series in Baltimore. They needed just one game to clinch the AL East. That may have sounded easy, but the Brewers found a way to make it difficult, surrendering the first three games. In the second-last game of the series, the Orioles beat the Brewers 11–3. After all the struggles of the early season and the remarkable push to first place after Kuenn's takeover, the future of the Brewers' season had all come down to one final game. Even the trip to the stadium became an absurd ordeal. Before the Brewers' bus had gone far from their suburban hotel, it was surrounded by Baltimore fans, waving brooms, trying to jam them through open windows, chanting "Sweep, Sweep, Sweep" to the Brewers within. The Brewers, a very loose collection of colorful personalities, managed to enjoy the attention.

Strangely, even though the Brewers were facing Jim Palmer, the Orioles' ace, the game itself turned out to be no contest, perhaps less perilous than the ride to the stadium. Don Sutton would prove to be equal to the task.

In the eighth inning, Baltimore's biggest fan appeared atop the Orioles' dugout and began leading the crowd in the shouted spelling of the team name. With each new letter, Wild Bill Hagy would twist himself into the closest imitation of the letter that he could manage. The contortions, the shouting, and the brooms were to no avail. The Orioles have the kind of fans that make it almost a special pleasure for other teams to beat them. The final score was 10–2. The Brewers had finally won the AL East. After the game, in the clubhouse, amid the traditional beer and champagne dousings, Molitor was more than jubilant. Taking his place before the rest of his half-dressed, champagne-soaked teammates, he began to repeat the cheer of Wild Bill Hagy. Twisting his body into the opening "O," Molitor went on to lead the Brewers through the Memorial Stadium spelling lesson, the shouting growing more raucous and the bending becoming funnier through it all: R I O L E S. It was the first pennant Molitor had managed to win since his days with the Gophers and the Bees. The Brewers had triumphed over their pitching woes and the American League East. They had even triumphed over the strange rituals of Baltimore fans.

It was a night for chants. Moose Haas led the team through a chant of B R E W E R S with the same comical body language. Then the Brewers were chanting M V P for Robin Yount. It could only make Yount angry, and Molitor thought Yount might slug someone. There was only one thing that mattered to Yount and that was winning the World Series.

The '82 Brewers had one of the greatest offensive ball clubs of recent decades. At the end of the regular season, the team had accumulated 891 runs, with Milwaukee players ranked first, second, and third in hits: Yount had 210, Cooper had 205, and Molitor had 201. Molitor led the American League with 136 runs scored, and Yount was in second place with 129. As leadoff hitter for the Brewers, Molitor had benefited from a potent lineup, including Gorman Thomas, who was tied with Reggie Jackson with a league leading 39 home runs. That year the Brewers had four players record over 100 RBIS: Yount, Cooper, Thomas, and Oglivie. Molitor's baserunning, of course, had contributed to the RBIS.

The pitching, too, bolstered by that late acquisition of Don Sutton, was much improved. Pete Vuckovich had the highest winning percentage in the American League. The Brewers had what they needed to contend.

COMING FROM BEHIND

It was as if that terrible early season and the last-minute clinch in Baltimore were giving the Brewers a taste for danger. Facing Gene Autry's California Angels in the American League Championship, they got off to a bad start. Perhaps still rattled by the strangeness of Baltimore — it was as if they had already played one cycle of playoffs — they didn't look good in their first real trip to the post-season. The Angels, anchored by Don Baylor, had playoff experience from the 1979 ALCS. In the past year they had acquired Reggie Jackson and, at the deadline, Tommy John. It was almost like facing the Yankees the year before.

In the first games in Anaheim, the experience told. Tommy John pitched a complete game to start the series with an 8–3 win, and in the second game, the Angels were again superior. Reggie Jackson, living up to his nickname of "Mr. October," homered in the third inning to make it 3–0, setting a playoff record for total RBIS and tying George Brett's record of six home runs in league championships. The Angels had scored another run in the fourth, making it 4–0. When the Brewers' Charlie Moore got to second in the fifth, Molitor came up to bat with two outs and hit what looked like a single to center field. Fred Lynn, the Angels' Gold Glove center fielder, missed the ball at his feet and it traveled to the center field fence. By the time Jackson, playing in right field, had recovered it and thrown it in, Molitor was blazing for home. It was only the second inside-the-park home run to be scored in playoff history. Molitor had made the game close, but not close enough, and the score of 4–2 would hold up.

The Angels' pitching had been the surprise. After the second game Molitor expressed his frustration. "I didn't expect [the Brewers] to come in here and score just five runs in two games. This club has too much offensive potential for that." Bruce Kison had held the middle of the Brewers' batting order — Cooper, Ted Simmons, Oglivie, and Thomas — hitless in 15 at bats during game two. The Brewers were going back to Milwaukee down 2–0 in a five-game series. No team had come back from that since the league playoffs had started in 1969. Molitor, however, was still willing to be positive. "We had two losses to use up and now both of them are used. It's plain and simple that we're faced with elimination and that they have three days before they have to face it. You simply can't get any closer than this to saying hello to the off-season. We've lost six of our last seven games, but on a positive note we're still only three games from the World Series."

Mirroring the series against the Yankees a year before, but this time playing on home territory, Molitor homered again in the third game, driving in the winning run for a 5–3 finish. Then the Brewers won the fourth game, making it another one-game series. Before the start of the final game, Molitor went over to the railing to embrace his father. Dick Molitor had driven down from St. Paul for the game, bringing five of

A. STAWICKI, THE TORONTO STAR

his daughters with him. He had saved vacation time to get away for the game, and he had saved more for the World Series.

It was a close, low-scoring game. Molitor doubled in the first to lead off and eventually got home. Oglivie homered in the fourth, but after six and a half innings, the Angels were leading 3–2. On the bench, Molitor was pumping his teammates. Cecil Cooper had had only two hits in 19 at bats. In the fifth inning, Cooper struck out with two men on base and two out. Molitor told him: "Cecil, your last at bat is going to be the most important one. You're going to get one more chance. Whether it's leading off an inning or with men on base, you're going to get one more chance." Cooper did. Batting in the seventh inning with bases loaded, he singled, scoring two runs. The Brewers won the game 4–3.

One of the UPI photos that appeared all over the world shows Paul Molitor, third baseman for a year, tagging Reggie Jackson as "Mr. October" slides head-first toward the base. Molitor had managed to play his first full season, 160 games, and the Brewers were going to the World Series.

Milwaukee was going to the World Series for the first time since Hank Aaron had led the Braves to the National League Pennant in 1957 and '58. Facing the Yankees in both World Series, the Braves had won the first and lost the second. The city was ready to celebrate.

THE 1982 WORLD SERIES

The Brewers and the Cardinals were a study in contrasts in 1982. The Brewers had scored the most home runs in the majors; the Cardinals, the fewest. Milwaukee baseball was built on big hits; St. Louis was built on very quick baserunning and excellent defense.

When they met the Cardinals in the first game in St. Louis, it was as if the hitters' frustrations with California's tight pitching had primed them for an explosion. Milwaukee chalked up 10 runs, while starter Mike Caldwell shut out the Cardinals. Molitor got five hits, a World Series record. Contact and hustle were responsible for his success. Three of the hits were in the infield, and a fourth was a short hit off a broken bat. The field might help the Cardinals, but there was at least one man on the Brewers who could capitalize on it. He was unaware that he was batting for a record when he went to bat in the ninth. "I didn't want to make the last out," Molitor said later. "I wanted to keep things going." After the game, a man from Cooperstown was in the clubhouse to collect the bat Molitor had used for the last two hits. One bat was broken, but the other one was going to the Hall of Fame. The next night, in a losing effort, Molitor managed two more hits, giving him another record for most hits in the first two games of a World Series.

When the series moved to Milwaukee, the city was ready to celebrate the Brewers as it never had before. Before game time there were tailgate parties in the stadium parking lot, as fans barbecued bratwurst and improvised picnics among the pickup trucks. If the Yankees and the Athletics had dominated the series for years, 1982 was a return to the heartland. The highest profile teams, the highest profile egos, and the biggest salaries in the game were out of the running. The Pabst True Blue Brew Crew cheerleaders were there to encourage the fans. Inside the stadium, bunting hung from the railings. For each successive day of the three games, a new attendance record would be established at County Stadium, eventually peaking at 55,562.

"We have good fans," said Molitor. "Usually at the World Series, you see a lot of high rollers, but these were our true fans. They ordered their tickets early so they could be here to see us. They helped us get here." Milwaukee had the feeling of a very large small town.

The Brewers lost the first home game and struggled through the first six innings of the next. In the seventh inning the crowd stood up and started singing, "Here we go, Brewers, here we go." Some pure spirit of baseball was alive in the crisp fall air. "I don't know if it bothered the Cardinals, but it had to help us," said Molitor. "They had been fairly quiet, with good reason, because we weren't playing very well. But they came to life in the seventh inning. They rose to their feet and kept things going." The Brewers responded with six runs in the inning, going on to win the game.

Then Milwaukee won game five by a score of 6–4, with Yount having his second four-hit game of the series. When the Brewers ended the home stand they had a 3–2 lead in games. Excited fans roared onto the field to tear up the bases. They wouldn't see the Brewers again until the victory parade.

But when the series moved back to St. Louis, the Brewers were having trouble putting it away. Game six, a repeat of the game two matchup between Don Sutton and rookie John Stuper, found Stuper masterful. The Cardinals won it 13–1. The Brewers struggled in the last game too. The Cardinals won the series in seven.

Through it all, Molitor thought they could come back, come back as they had against Baltimore, come back as they had, miraculously, against the Angels. "We dipped into that well so many times for dramatic victories. I thought we could do it one more time, but we couldn't. Look around this clubhouse," Molitor invited a reporter. "Nobody is hanging their head between their legs. That's the kind of club we are. We never got cocky in victory, and now we aren't going to hang our heads in shame. I'm going home with my head high."

"Harvey's Wallbangers" lost to a team built on a different principle. The Brewers depended on homers, the Cardinals didn't. The Cardinals had opted for speed. Busch Stadium in St. Louis had very quick astroturf, and the Cardinals benefited from playing four of the seven games there, winning three at home and just one in County Stadium. Lonnie Smith and Keith Hernandez were particularly quick, but many of the Cardinals were adept at stealing bases. It was an area of the game in which only Molitor and Yount could compete. Molitor has always savored the ironies of his career, but there was one he would avoid: the Brewers had lost the World Series to a team that played his kind of baseball, the team that had first drafted him back in 1974.

There is no glory in sport like winning the World Series. Even the Super Bowl, a single championship game played at a neutral site, pales by comparison. The national media attention and the excitement of the fans fill the World Series with incredible tension. The isolation of the pitcher and the batter is never so intense. A fielder's play never counts for so much. Finally, there is nothing quite like the sense of loss that comes when a team sees victory slip through their fingers. They can console themselves with the thought that only two teams can be good enough to get there and someone has to be second best, but it is hard to escape the weight of defeat. A hitter will remember pitches that he might have swung on, swings that might have been better, plays that if played a bit differently would have changed the way he will forever view his career.

For Molitor in 1982, however, there was very little of this. He was only 26, was recently married, and had just managed to play his first full season of baseball. The Brewers had won the second half of the AL East in 1981, and they had made it to the 1982 World Series when no one expected them to, even overcoming a two game deficit against the Angels in their first trip to the post-season. The Brewers at the end of 1982 were a far better club than they had ever been before. With Harvey Kuenn managing, they were a far better team than they had been at the start of the season. Molitor, whose own performance had been remarkable, had every reason to expect to be back in the post-season in the near future. He had set hitting records in the first two games, laying the foundations of an extraordinary post-season batting career that he would be able to build on in the years to come.

When the Brewers returned home to Milwaukee, there was a parade down Wisconsin Avenue. The players traveled in glistening vintage convertibles — Auburns, Cords, Packards — through throngs of cheering fans. The cars spoke of a Golden Age. Ten thousand people awaited the Brewers in County Stadium, cheering for a team who weren't losers, a team who had only really started to compete.

6

Looking to the Future

At the beginning of the 1983 season, the Brewers and Paul Molitor were finally interested in the same kind of contract at the same time. Molitor was only a year away from free agency, and the Brewers were anxious to avoid those waters. Molitor was interested in staying in Milwaukee. The string of one-year contracts was coming to an end. "I was more concerned about what was going to make Paul and Linda Molitor happy," he admitted, after the deal was signed. "There's no question we wanted to stay here, and that's very important in itself. One of the keys I'm happiest with is for the first three years, there's no trade. We wanted to stay in Milwaukee. We wanted to at least provide that for the first three years, with limited trade on the last two years."

The contract was for five years. There was a signing bonus of $300,000, and regular salaries of $700,000 for 1983, $900,000 for 1984 and '85, and $1.1 million in '86 and '87. There was a bonus of $25,000 for playing in 130 games, another $25,000 if he appeared in 145 games, and another $25,000 if he reached 625 appearances at the plate. If Molitor were traded in 1986, he would receive $500,000 from the Brewers, $200,000 if he were traded in 1987. Even without the incentives, the contract had a total value of $5 million.

Speaking for the Brewers, general manager Harry Dalton said: "We're very pleased. I hope he plays his entire career in Milwaukee. Because of his age and the fact he's already established at 26, he's a fellow we can look to in our future for 10 years, perhaps."

Molitor, too, was looking to the future. "The first five years you kind of get yourself established and your confidence level increases. The next five years, at least in my case, should be my best years. I'm physically maturing. I'm mentally maturing. As far as time and potential, I think from 26 to 30 I should be at my highest peak."

Looking back on his first full season of play, Molitor continued: "I'm hoping last year is indicative of things to come, mostly in the guise that I can be an everyday player. I don't have to be rested, and I can remain strong in September. I'm looking to become known as an everyday player."

Molitor performed well in '83, playing in 152 games, but it wasn't the season he was looking for. His defense improved, but his batting average fell from .302 in '82 to .270. Through part of the season he was plagued with a mysterious hand injury, a broken bone in his wrist that resisted diagnosis.

The team that had taken Milwaukee to the World Series gradually dissolved. Rollie Fingers, who had had a league-leading 28 saves in the strike shortened season of '81, and 29 saves in the pennant-winning season, was out with elbow surgery for 1983. Homerun king Gorman Thomas left in July, and the Brewers were relieved to see him go. Thomas had become increasingly difficult to work with, and his slipshod attitude caused problems for the team and presented a poor model for younger players. Molitor's relationship with him had been a difficult one, but he retained some respect for Thomas, both as a player and a person.

The Brewers' glorious run production of 1982 sagged badly in '83, falling from 891 to 764. In the very tough American

Giving an anti-drug talk at a Milwaukee school.
THE MILWAUKEE JOURNAL

League East, the Brewers tumbled from first to fifth place in a wild race for second with Detroit, New York, and Toronto.

A DISASTROUS YEAR REDEEMED

The 1984 season started badly. Molitor was suffering serious difficulties with his right elbow that made playing difficult, almost impossible. He played in only 13 games at the start of the season, managing 10 hits. He was batting .217. Surgery would be necessary and it couldn't be put off. By May 2, he was through for the season.

The type of operation Molitor required was first performed on pitcher Tommy John in 1974, and it involved the reconstruction of the elbow using transplanted tendons. The year would be spent in recovery and rehabilitation.

In the second week of May, another problem surfaced, one that Molitor thought he had put behind him. In the trial of a Milwaukee drug dealer, Tony Peters, five members of the Brewers were named as customers. Molitor was among them. When questioned about it by the press, Molitor was unable to answer — it was a part of his past that he'd fought to overcome, and he hadn't expected it to resurface now.

Molitor's fortunes were closely intertwined with those of the Brewers, and there would be no comfort for him in how the team fared in his absence. At the end of 1984, the Brewers finished last in the American League East, just two years after an appearance in the World Series. The fall from 1983 had been precipitous: in a year, the winning percentage dropped from .537 to .416. They were 36 1/2 games back of the first-place Detroit Tigers. The numbers were as bad as they had been in 1977. Total run production had fallen another 123 to 641. One would have to go back to 1970, the Brewers' first season, to find numbers that were worse. Perennial cellar dwellers from their inception, the Brewers had built themselves into a fine team by the early '80s, only to see it disappear in a single season.

Throughout the year, however, Molitor's spirits remained high. He had always cared deeply about family, and now he and his wife were expecting their first child. On October 25, 1984, Linda Molitor gave birth to their daughter Blaire. The new baby would more than redeem the year for Molitor, putting an otherwise disastrous series of events in perspective.

AN ALL-STAR IN MINNEAPOLIS

At spring training in 1985, Molitor was just happy to be playing. There was some question about how the reconstructed elbow would perform, so that every time Molitor threw the ball, management and coaches would fear the worst. But the elbow was up to the task of throwing as well as hitting. When the season began, Molitor was back in the leadoff spot in the batting order and back into the game as the regular third baseman. His throws from third were hard and accurate. The elbow still needed some extra rest. It meant not playing in the infield in every fifth game, but even then Molitor was in the lineup as designated hitter.

Molitor's comeback was quick, and he was soon leading the Brewers in batting average. He was inspired being back, and he was inspired knowing what his absence had meant to the team. At midseason he was picked to go to the All-Star Game. After missing the game in 1980 and the season in 1984, it was going to be very special for him.

The 1985 All-Star Game was played in Minneapolis, just across the river from St. Paul. It was a wonderful homecoming, playing in the Hubert H. Humphrey Metrodome with family and friends in the stands. It was a chance to celebrate what the Twin Cities area had come to mean to baseball. Molitor was reunited on the American League team with two other St. Paul natives who were carving out brilliant careers: Dave Winfield and Jack Morris. It was a chance to reminisce in the spotlight about boyhood teams and coaches, about American Legion ball, the Gophers, and Dick Siebert.

Molitor was out of the lineup for two weeks in August with a bad ankle sprain, and the Brewers had another losing season, but it was a year of personal satisfaction. He had managed to play in 140 games and his .297 batting average led the team. In a season in which Robin Yount had missed 39 games, Molitor and Cecil Cooper had carried the offense.

"THE WORST THING YOU CAN DO"

Nineteen eighty-six began positively. Molitor had a good spring training camp, and the elbow was better than ever. With Cooper and Yount having problems with various injuries, Molitor was the healthiest member of the Brewers' star infield. The team had a talented-looking group of pitching prospects, and Molitor was looking forward to a good season with a team that was rebuilding.

Then, on May 9, charging a bunt in Oakland, Molitor partially tore his right hamstring. He was disappointed but philosophical. "You wonder why you have to go through injuries. I take care of myself. Some things happen that you have no control over. It's the nature of the game. Hopefully, I can get back as soon as possible. You have to give it time to heal. The worst thing you can do is try to come back too soon. Then, if you hurt it, you're out a month."

Coming back too soon might be the worst thing an injured player could do, but that season Molitor did it. He was back in the lineup three weeks later, on May 30, playing in left field in Cleveland. Molitor always returned from the disabled list ready to explode at the plate. He led off the first inning with a home run against Phil Niekro, and later hit two singles and collected three RBIS. The next day he aggravated the injury, played the day after as DH, and was then back on the DL.

Yes, coming back too soon was the worst thing anyone could do, but then Molitor did it again. Back from the disabled list on June 17, playing in Toronto, he tore the right hamstring again as he chased a ball in left field. The next day, he took himself out of the lineup after struggling through the first three innings. He would be out of the lineup for a further three weeks.

"When I came back against Toronto, I thought it was all behind me. I've never had experience with hamstrings before. This is all new to me. You can't judge it by pain. Before Toronto I was pain free for a week and hurt it my first game back. That's the toughest part. In game situations, the adrenaline gets flowing. You go on instinct. You can simulate game conditions as best you can, but it's not the same."

When Molitor came back the third time, on July 16, the right hamstring didn't feel as good as it had after the second comeback. Maybe that was the key. Whatever it was, he was back to stay this time, somehow managing to remain reasonably healthy. He was in good enough shape to be back at his almost regular position at third, and by mid-August he was sound enough to be making bunt plays at third without difficulty.

Back in Cleveland on August 19, Molitor had one of the greatest games of his career. He homered to lead off the first inning, doubled and scored in the third, sacrifice bunted in the fifth, homered in the eighth, and doubled in the ninth to score another run. At third base, he made a leaping catch in the third inning on a line drive to start a double play, then made running, bare-handed catches on bunts in the eighth and ninth innings.

In the glory days of "Harvey's Wallbangers," that performance might have ignited a 15-run assault. In 1986 the Brewers were so desperate and nostalgic they'd even brought back Gorman Thomas as designated hitter. That night in Cleveland, Molitor's performance was almost all the offense the Brewers had. He got four of the club's eight hits, scored three runs and brought in another in a game the Brewers won 5–3.

7

Streaks

The 1987 season began with tremendous change and promise for the Brewers. The preceding year had started with changes and it had ended with more of them. The decline that had started right after the trip to the World Series had to be halted. Of the 40 players on the team roster at the end of the '85 season, only eight remained at the beginning of 1987. Of the players who had gone to the series in '82, only Molitor, Yount, Gantner, and Cooper remained. Molitor felt the turnover was "something that had to be done," but "you never knew how quick it would happen. It was so dramatic. A lot of players came and went in a hurry." The veterans would feel the burden of leadership.

There was reason to be excited. The season opened with a win, and then the Brewers seemed to keep on winning. By April 14 the Brewers had put together a seven-game streak. That night, in his customary leadoff spot, Molitor opened the game with a home run. It was the most fun he'd had playing baseball in three or four years. The mood of the team was almost giddy. For Molitor it was a chance to put the previous seasons behind him. "So much is said about the mental aspect of the game," he told reporter Tom Flaherty. "Right now, we're so positive."

You could count the excitement in County Stadium. After six home games, attendance hovered around 180,000, a full 82,000 more fans than had turned up for the first six games of 1986. As the wins accumulated, the Brewers went by the Oakland A's 1981 American League record of 11 wins at the beginning of a season, eventually tying the 1982 13-game winning streak of the National League's Atlanta Braves. The night they tied the Braves' record in Comiskey Park, April 20, Flaherty estimated half the crowd had come from Wisconsin for the game. As the national media attention became intense, Molitor was concerned to defuse the tension. "These are fun games. There's some pressure, but it's a different kind of pressure. If the streak ends, it's not the end of the world. We just have to be thankful and keep things in perspective." It was important to keep your eye on what counted, and what counted was the end of the season, not the beginning. "With a start like this, it would be a real disappointment if the Brewers don't stay in the race. How do you assess a 13-game winning streak? Who knows? We're 13 games over .500. If we win the pennant by one game, this 13th game will be very important. But that's a long way off." Molitor knew just what a streak could mean. The '81 A's had gone to the ALCS. The '82 Braves had gone to the NLCS. Some of the pressure on the Brewers came from controlling the excitement that a winning streak — and knowledge of where it might lead — could generate.

The streak ended at 13, but the Brewers came right back, winning their next four games before a loss to Oakland. Then on April 29, in the 20th game of the season, Molitor was caught in a rundown in the first inning, hurting his right hamstring. He had the injury wrapped and stayed in the game. In the second inning, at bat again, he connected for a homer. "When I hit the ball, I pushed out of the batter's box. I felt it right away." He had suffered a pull in the right hamstring, the same injury that had put him on the disabled list in 1986. He didn't think it was serious, but he would be out for four weeks.

At the end of the streak, Molitor had a batting average of .370. At the time of the injury he had pushed the average to .395. He was leading the American League with 23 runs, 32 hits, and nine doubles. His nine stolen bases were second in the league.

With Molitor out, the fortunes of the 18–2 Brewers went directly into reverse, with the team developing a 12-game losing streak. By the time Molitor returned, the Brewers had gone 4–16. Since he'd joined the team, Molitor had had an impact on the Brewers' ability to win, but in 1987, with a young and untested roster, he meant far more than he had ever meant before. With Molitor in the lineup the Brewers scored an average of 6.9 runs per game. With him out, the average was 2.9. The team had somehow dropped from playing .900 ball to playing .200.

When he came back from the hamstring injury, it wasn't because it was better. He was frustrated being out of the game and upset by the way things were going with the team. He didn't think the injury was going "to feel better any time soon," so he was ready to play. The return was short-lived and problem-filled. A week after his return, he limped off the field again. Fielding a grounder, he had felt his right leg tightening. Then he pulled a groin muscle running the bases. Molitor, a player who had long turned singles into doubles, turned a triple into a double. The hamstring injury was leading to other injuries, as Molitor soon realized: "A lot of times when you have a muscle pull, other muscles compensate, and they give way too." Later in June he missed a game in Boston with a swollen elbow. The elbow was drained, but three days later the swelling was back. Then, on June 26, he reinjured the hamstring, and he was out for another three weeks.

On July 16, in the first game after the All-Star break, Molitor returned to active duty from the disabled list for the second time in the season. It was as if the season were starting all over again. Recurring elbow problems would keep him from playing in the infield. He would be replacing Cecil Cooper at the designated hitter spot, something Molitor regretted. In four at bats against California that day, he managed a single hit, a run scoring-double in the second inning. Then, on a single by Ernest Riles, Molitor was surprised to get the signal to run home. The ball got away from the catcher, but Molitor thought he would have made it anyway. The legs were definitely working again. His single hit in the game was the beginning of many to come.

Ten days later, with the Brewers facing Oakland in County Stadium, Molitor led off with a single. While Riles was at bat, Molitor stole second. When Riles grounded out to the Oakland pitcher, Dennis Lamp, Molitor stole third. After Robin Yount walked, the two Milwaukee stars managed to complete a double steal. The Oakland catcher threw to second in a failed attempt to catch Yount, and Molitor exploded towards home, sliding head first to the plate and beating the return throw from second. He'd managed to steal second, third, and home in a single inning, the first time it had been done in the American League since Dave Nelson had done it for the Texas Rangers on August 30, 1974.

In fact, the feat is pretty rare in baseball history. When Molitor did it, it was just the 33rd time it had happened in the history of the majors, and only the sixth time anyone had managed it since 1928. When Pete Rose did it in 1980, it was the first time it had happened in the National League in 52 years. Three men — Honus Wagner, Max Carey, and Jack Tavener — had managed to do it twice, and one, Ty Cobb, had managed to do it three times, but those were names from the mythic past of the game, when anything had been possible. Three American Leaguers had done it in 1912, Cobb and Shoeless Joe Jackson among them, and, in 1915, three American Leaguers and a National League player had managed it. Molitor was beginning to flirt with the achievements of legends.

After the triple steal, Molitor doubled in the second and tripled in the eighth inning. It was the third game in a row that he had three hits in five at bats. He had hit safely in every game since his return and had a batting average of .452 for the period. The DH position was allowing him a single-minded concentration on offense. He was doing a lot of extra batting practice, making up for the frustrating layoffs. He was already conscious of the ten-game streak: "You know it's not going to last, but you want to keep it up as long as possible."

The next night, against the Rangers in Arlington, manager Tom Trebelhorn tried to take greater advantage of Molitor's RBI potential by moving him from first to third in the order. It didn't work, and Molitor went 1 for 4 in a 5–4 loss. Returned to the leadoff spot the next night, Molitor had two runs, stole two bases, and hit a three-run homer. The leadoff spot was where Molitor wanted to be, and it seemed to be where he performed best. He counted on Yount following him, knew Yount's timing, knew exactly what he could do. "I think I belong in the leadoff spot, at least against right-handed pitchers. I think our best lineup is with me and Robin at the top." On a team with more offensive talent, with more contact hitters and better base runners, Trebelhorn would have been right, but given the team as it was, Molitor belonged in the leadoff spot. He would set the tone for the game, rattle an opposing pitcher, and possibly gain an extra at bat in the closing innings.

Then, in game after game, win or lose, Molitor kept finding ways to hit safely. Once he reached 20 straight games, people started to pay attention. In Chicago, on August 9, he had to wait until the ninth inning to get his hit. It was the 24th game in a row, and he had tied the Brewers' record set by Dave May in 1973. He was trying to defuse the pressure, trying to keep his emphasis on the team. "It wears a little bit on you mentally. It's something you can't help but be aware of. People are noticing it, your teammates and everything. To be honest, I say a little prayer before each game to help me concentrate on helping our team win a ball game first of all, and as far as personal goals, let them fall where they may."

Of coming to bat hitless in the ninth, he said, "You're aware of your personal situation at that time, but you try to keep your focus on what you're trying to do. And in that situation, we needed to get some more runs on the board."

Molitor's streak was already being mentioned in the context of the two longest streaks in baseball — Joe DiMaggio's 56-game streak in 1941 and Pete Rose's 44-game streak in 1978 — but Molitor remained cautious. "It's hard to imagine hitting in that many games at this level. Even Rose. It's a tough daily grind, and it wears on you mentally. It helps me appreciate those men." The 25th-game hit the next night established a new club record. The night after, Molitor went 3 for 4, but it was in a losing cause. His only comment was, "It's a lot more fun when you're winning."

In the 28th game, Molitor faced Baltimore's Mike Boddicker, a pitcher he'd known for a long time and who had special luck against him. Molitor had a .136 average against Boddicker with three hits in 22 at bats. The two men had first encountered one another when they were high school students playing in the American Legion League. Molitor had been pitching then, when St. Paul had faced Cedar Rapids. Cedar Rapids had won 2–1 in the tenth inning. They'd met again later when Molitor played for the University of Minnesota and Boddicker pitched for the University of Iowa. Boddicker had several good pitches and always presented special problems for Molitor. Boddicker called his best pitch a "foshball," a blooping fastball that behaved like a screwball and which had a way of baffling hitters. True to form, Boddicker kept Molitor o for 4 until he left the game. Then Molitor seized his chance and hit a home run off the relief pitcher.

What was remarkable about the streak to this point wasn't just the streak itself — it was the quality of production Molitor had maintained. During those 28 games, Molitor had managed to carry a .422 average with six home runs and 26 RBIs.

The next night, Molitor was hitless until he managed a single in the seventh inning. "I looked like a guy with a 28 game hitless streak," he thought afterward. A player has to have some lucky days to keep a streak alive, and this was one of them. The next day he pushed it to 30, still against Baltimore, but it was in a losing cause. He opened the game with a single, but in the fifth inning hit into a fielder's choice that got B.J. Surhoff out at home plate. The Brewers lost by a score of 2–1. "It's always nice to get the hit early to stop the distraction that the streak can be. But it's tough to think about a streak when you lose a tough game like this."

When it didn't help the team, the streak was disturbing. Molitor couldn't celebrate his hit when another at bat had helped cost Milwaukee the game. It was the worst sort of attention. Molitor was working through a bad patch in his hitting, but his contact was so good that the streak was still alive. His real concern was the number of games that separated Milwaukee from Toronto in the standings. At times the media attention that the streak was generating bothered him. It was as if he was supposed to celebrate a personal accomplishment when he was hitting badly in a game that his team lost.

Molitor had passed a milestone when he hit the 30-game mark. That was the point where a hitting streak really started to count. When he hit in the 31st game, still against Baltimore, he tied Ken Landreaux's 1980 streak, the longest streak of the decade. He had both a single and a double in that game, and the Brewers had won. "I've been a bit overanxious," he admitted about the spotty hitting that the streak had survived. "I just need to relax more. Thirty or 31 doesn't have that much significance, but each day you squeeze a hit out you have a chance to do something you may never do again." As long as the Brewers won, Molitor was happy. That was the only thing that let him enjoy the streak. "The ironic thing about this is that there's so much attention brought to a streak like this. But once it's over, it's gone. It's something that you enjoy and just ride it until it ends. I'm really not looking forward to it ending. I know that it will. But it won't be the end of the world or the end of my season by any means. It's something that I've had fun with so I'd like to keep it going as long as possible. When it ends it'll be disappointing but you have to pick up and start again the next day."

Molitor was suddenly getting national attention. There was a feature in *Sports Illustrated* after the 31st hit, and he was getting calls from the television networks for interviews. The *Washington Post* had a reporter following the Brewers for the duration of the streak.

The hit for game 32 was a perfect bunt down the third base line in Cleveland. During the previous games in Baltimore, the third baseman had played Molitor so closely that the idea of a bunt had been more in the minds of the Orioles than it had in Molitor's. In Cleveland, the Indians' third baseman was playing well back, and Molitor took advantage of it. Hit 33 came the next night on his fourth at bat, in the sixth inning, when he managed to get to first on an infield grounder. He had the longest streak since Rose and the longest streak in the American League since Dom DiMaggio had a run of 34 games in 1949. Molitor's name was moving up a list littered with legends. At 33 games, he was in a three-way tie with Rogers Hornsby and Heinie Manush.

When Molitor went into the 34th game, he loosened up. The flukes that had gotten him through the bad patch weren't needed. He hit a three-run homer in the fourth inning and then went on to get a double and two singles for his first four-hit game of the season, pushing his average for the streak back up to .417. He was in a four-way tie for 11th place with Dom DiMaggio and George McQuinn, who had done it in 1938, and with George Sisler's 1925 streak. "It's an honor to be among those names. They're some of the greatest names in baseball," he remarked.

Molitor wasn't just pleased to be among legends. He was back on his game. "I'd been getting a little away from my game. I'm sure it stems from, in the back of my mind, the streak. It's hard to put it out of your mind. I was able to concentrate more after the homer — get in some good swings." When Molitor hit like that, he was winning games, not just keeping the streak alive. The next night, still in Cleveland, he hit two doubles and a single, tying a 35-game streak by Ty Cobb in 1917. The road trip was over. The Brewers were going home to County Stadium, and the streak was still alive.

As the streak gradually built momentum, Molitor's teammates were sounding more excited about it than Molitor seemed. "I'd be lying if I said I didn't think about it," Rob Deer confessed. "It's a relief when he gets a hit. It's such a great thing he's got going. You hate to see it end." Deer could feel the pressure on the team that was being generated by the streak. "I feel the tension, so I know he does," admitted the outfielder. "I don't think people realize the pressure, not only to get a hit but to keep your mind off it during the day. But Paul's a different person. If anybody can handle it, he can. He's the same all the time."

Molitor is fond of saying there's no pressure in situations

where there is terrific pressure. It's as if it's a formula, a technique for self-hypnosis, one more way of bringing all his concentration to the ball flying towards him at 90 miles an hour. He watches that ball, thinks about it, longer than anyone might expect him to. Molitor does not rise to pressure — he rises above it. He rises to some pure joy in the game when it is played as hard and as well as it can be.

It wasn't just the streak that was affecting Milwaukee's play. It was Molitor's attitude to the game. Deer said, "Whenever he does something, you just hope he gets up. You can look at his knees right now. He's got strawberries all over them. It's always that way." After hitting in the 32nd game, Molitor had been hit by a pitch, hurting his left tricep. His name wasn't on the roster for the next game until he'd decided the muscle was loose enough to play. Every night, Molitor was putting aside the ongoing problems that had plagued his season. He wasn't going out to maintain his remarkable streak — he was going out to help the Brewers win baseball games.

Reliever Dan Plesac expressed the team's respect: "Everybody's pulling for him. Paul's a unique guy — a real team player. You like good things to happen to him." Every time Molitor would get another hit, Plesac would say, "The beat goes on." Rick Manning described the feeling. "It keeps us pumped up. If he doesn't get it in this at bat, we say, 'Let's go. Get him some more at bats.'" That was the key to it. Molitor wouldn't allow himself to enjoy the streak if the team didn't win, so the team was in part working to win to help feed the streak. "First and foremost we're thinking about winning the game, and I know it's that way with Paulie, too," said Manning.

The streak was an emblem of how hard Molitor worked and how much he cared about the team winning. When Molitor was in the lineup, it wasn't just his talent that was contributing to Brewers' victories, it was the way he would put his body on the line stealing bases, the way he'd run out a hit, the way he wouldn't celebrate anything but winning. The few remaining veterans on the Brewers had always wanted to win, but Molitor was demonstrating to all the new recruits how much it mattered and how it could be done.

It wasn't just on the field that Molitor was there for his teammates. He was there for them with the management and in the press. Listed to play in center field against Cleveland in 1986, he had talked to the manager about putting Rick Manning at center against his old team, getting Manning an opportunity to shine. Early in the season, when the Brewers had reached 11 games in their winning streak, Rob Deer was leading the American League in homers and RBIS. Molitor said of him, "When he gets in a groove, he can carry our ballclub, and he's probably the only guy on the team who can do that." That was what made Molitor so special. He'd go out of his way to compliment other players in the press, always spreading the credit around when the team was successful.

THE BEAT GOES ON

When the Brewers got back to Milwaukee, they could see what the streak and the attention meant to the club and to the fans. At County Stadium there were buttons for sale with Molitor's picture and the current number of the streak. On August 21 there was a standing ovation for Molitor before the first game started, from 37,431 people. The size of the crowd was incredible, especially for a rainy night. "I was quite nervous. I was more jittery. It was difficult to calm myself down," Molitor would say later. Bringing the streak home to Milwaukee was particularly rewarding. "That first at bat was very special to me. I'll probably remember that more than any other part of this streak." The hit for game 36 didn't come with that first at bat. It came in the form of a double in the fourth inning against Danny Jackson and the Royals. It was the first Milwaukee hit of the night. Kansas City's George Brett, who had once had a streak of 30 and had once pursued the elusive .400 batting average, offered his congratulations, and there was another standing ovation from the crowd.

The next day was Molitor's 31st birthday, August 22, 1987. He spent the morning with his family. In the midst of his sudden celebrity, Molitor was maintaining family rituals, trying to insulate himself from the pressure. "It was kind of nice, a little birthday lunch with my wife and daughter, of course, and my mom and three of my sisters and another friend from the Twin Cities were down. We just kind of sat around and took it easy. We had some cake, opened some presents. Nothing special, the usual birthday stuff."

That night, a few hundred more supporters had found their way to the Brewers' game. Attendance was 37,740, and there were banners wishing him "Happy Birthday." Before the game, he was interviewed for ABC's *Wide World of Sports* and was named their athlete of the week.

As he walked toward the plate to lead off in the first, there was a standing ovation. He connected with a fastball on Bret Saberhagen's 1–2 pitch and got to first base as the crowd rose to their feet and gave him another standing ovation. George Brett was there to congratulate him again. They talked about how nice it was to get the hit out of the way early when you were having a streak. Then Brett told Molitor that Saberhagen had a good pickoff move just as Saberhagen threw quickly to first and managed to pick Molitor off. That was baseball. You had to keep your mind in the game. You couldn't think too much about a streak.

At the end of the inning, the public address system broadcast Sonny and Cher singing "The Beat Goes On." The streak even had a theme song. The scoreboard showed pictures of the men who had had longer streaks. Molitor had just tied the 37-game streak that Tommy Holmes had recorded with the Boston Braves in 1945. Only four men were ahead of him now: Ty Cobb, at 40, George Sisler, at 41, then Pete Rose and Joe DiMaggio.

The next night he reached 38 to take sole possession of fifth place on the list. After a day off, he made it 39, one short of Ty Cobb's streak of 1911. On Wednesday, August 26, the Brewers faced Cleveland rookie John Farrell. The game turned into a pitchers' duel between Farrell and Ted Higuera. Molitor managed to reach base in the eighth, but he did it on an error, not a recorded hit. After nine innings the game was tied at zero and Molitor didn't have a hit.

Farrell retired after nine innings and reliever Doug Jones took over in the bottom of the tenth. Rob Deer was hit by a pitch and Mike Felder went in to run for him. The next batter grounded out, moving Felder to second. Jones then walked Dale Sveum intentionally, putting runners at first and second. Tom Trebelhorn sent in veteran Rick Manning as a pinch hitter, while Molitor waited in the on deck circle. Molitor told Manning, "Come on, get a hit." Manning wanted to say, "I'll get an infield hit." Thinking about the streak, and the possibility that Manning might not drive in a run, Molitor was conscious of the irony of the situation: "To possibly have an extra chance because of the ineptitude of our offense." When Manning took a called strike from Jones, there were some cheers in the stadium. Manning hit the next pitch for a single. As Felder took off from second, Molitor stood up with his arms raised, signaling Felder to come home standing up. The Brewers had won the game 1–0. The streak was over.

The stadium was silent except for a sprinkling of boos. Molitor ran to first base to congratulate Manning. All Manning could say was "Sorry." Molitor said, "Sorry?" Then the team was rushing to congratulate Molitor and Manning. The

11,000 fans who had sat in the rain throughout the game remained to applaud Molitor, standing and clapping, yelling to call him out of the dugout. For Molitor it was the most emotional moment of the streak, and he was visibly moved by the ovation.

"It reminds me of what I've been through, and it humbles you," Molitor explained afterwards. "I just thank God for the opportunity to do it. The fact that it's in the top five or six hitting streaks in the history of the game makes you realize that you're very fortunate to have this. It's been a great experience. I enjoyed this. I'm sure my pride will continue to grow as the years pass. Someday, when I quit playing, I'm sure I'll look back and realize it was one of my best personal achievements as far as the game is concerned." Years later, he would find himself remembering those pitches that he faced in the fortieth game, wondering if there was anything he might have done differently.

The end had to come some time, and when it did it came the best way it could: at home and in a winning effort. It was only at the end that Molitor could appreciate what he had done, and it was only at the end that others could let him know what it had meant to be a part of it. Tony Moser, the team's hitting instructor, wrapped his arm around Molitor and told him it was the greatest thing he had had a chance to see in sports.

Talking about the game afterwards, Molitor didn't blame it on the weather. He gave the credit to John Farrell, who had ended the streak in just his second major league game. After the game, Farrell asked Molitor to autograph a baseball for him.

Throughout the streak, Molitor had said how it made him appreciate more the players who had gone further before him. In the final 10 days of the streak, he had found himself more and more at the center of a spotlight that he had never previously been in. He had faced a press conference before and

Molitor is cheered by family members at Met Stadium,
(left to right) Paul's father Dick, his sister Vicki Devincenzi,
her friend Jill Pearce, and his mother Kathy.

CRAIG BORCK, ST. PAUL PIONEER PRESS

after every game, and the attention was disorienting—he had felt like it was happening to someone else. At the end of the streak, when the Brewers' victory had kept him from another at bat and the crowd had fallen silent, he felt the strangeness particularly. For Molitor it was a "distortion of reality" when one player's achievement could even take precedence over the team winning.

The next afternoon he was back at County Stadium to face the Indians again. He had said he would start over again the day after the streak ended and he did. He hit a double and a single and stole a base. The way Molitor was hitting in 1987, it was as if game 40 had been the fluke, not the fact that he'd run the streak to 39.

In a season in which he missed 44 games due to injuries, more than a quarter of the season, Molitor produced totals that were extraordinary. He led the American League in doubles, 41, scored more runs than any other player, 114, and had the second highest batting average, with .353 to Wade Boggs's .363. He had also approached Joe DiMaggio in another aspect of the game: in those weird statistics that baseball loves to keep, he was then tied for second place behind DiMaggio for highest season batting average by an American league right-handed batter since DiMaggio's .357 in 1941. Molitor also managed a career-high 45 stolen bases that year. That he hit for a mere 75 RBIS can be credited to his hitting first in the Brewers' lineup, and to the fact that he played in only 118 games.

The hitting streak is almost the harshest test of a hitter's abilities, and it shows in the names of the few men who have managed to run them longer than Molitor did. An average can always be pumped up another day, but the streak depends on getting a hit no matter who is pitching, no matter how one might feel on a particular day. Off days aren't allowed on a hitting streak. It's the ultimate accomplishment for a contact hitter, evidence that he can find a way to hit against almost any pitcher that the majors might throw at him.

By 1987, Molitor's constant attention to his swing was resulting in continued improvement. The designated hitter role, dictated for much of 1987 by his hamstring injuries, bothered him. He wanted to contribute more, to feel part of the team and part of the game, but the DH role freed him for the first time from the constant position shifting that had interfered with his career in Milwaukee in so many previous seasons. Though he still continued to swing at first pitches — a sign of his aggressiveness at the plate — he was a model of concentrated energy, facing the pitcher with an absolute minimum of movement. His judgement of pitches was sharper than it had ever been, and his wrist speed was explosive.

A hitting streak is a personal accomplishment. A team can benefit, but the streak does not in itself make the difference between winning and losing. Molitor has always focused on team accomplishments, since his days in college ball with the Gophers and in the minors when he decided to stay with the Burlington Bees back in 1977. More remarkable than the streak is what Molitor's bat and his presence meant to his team. During the 1987 season, he was literally the difference between winning and losing for the Brewers. That year the best and worst winning percentages in major league baseball were in the American League East, with Detroit at .605 and Cleveland at .377. The Brewers finished third, seven games behind Detroit and five behind the Toronto Blue Jays, who had collapsed in the final week of the regular season after both Tony Fernandez and Ernie Whitt had suffered injuries. The Brewers ended with a creditable .562, better than any team in either the AL West or NL West.

The most important stats for Molitor are those that show his contribution to team performance. At one point in August, near the end of his hitting streak, the Brewers were 47–26 with Molitor in the lineup, and 14–30 when he was on the disabled list. In percentage terms, the Brewers were, by mid-August, a .644 team when Molitor was in the lineup and a .318 team when he wasn't. From mid-August to the end of the season, with Molitor managing to stay healthy, Milwaukee's overall winning percentage increased from .521 to the final .562, and the winning percentage with Molitor in the lineup got even better after the streak had ended. With Molitor in the lineup, they were 77–41 for the season, with a winning percentage of .653. If these stats need any more emphasis, consider that Molitor played half of the year as designated hitter and in that role could only influence team offense, not defense. His presence was such that the team managed to improve even after his play slumped during September. At least statistically, it isn't overstating the case to say that the '87 Brewers with Molitor in the lineup could be considered the best team in baseball; without him, the worst. That doesn't mean they could have won the ALCS, but in the daily grind of the season, Molitor was able to make the Brewers a far more fiercely competitive baseball team than they could possibly have been without him.

At the end of the '87 season, Paul Molitor would have as many MVP votes as he'd ever receive as a Brewer. He was in fifth place. So much for a small-market team that wasn't winning its division. That year Toronto's George Bell would be MVP.

Ron Simon hoped that the prominence Molitor had gained from the hitting streak might translate into opportunities for endorsements, but few presented themselves. The attention brought by the streak was a transitory fame, and Molitor settled comfortably into the customary rhythms of Milwaukee life. In November, he appeared at the opening of a ham store as part of a club promotion. Later the Molitors appeared smiling in a *Milwaukee Magazine* advertisement, declaring "We love our *Original American Closets*. They are the Big League closet company in Milwaukee."

8

Life in Milwaukee

Following the 1987 season, Paul and Linda Molitor decided to make their winter home in Milwaukee, after spending the previous four winters in California. It was a sign of Molitor's commitment to his family and to the city he worked in. Paul Molitor is almost as exceptional a person as he is a baseball player, and as his career developed he became increasingly active in community service as well as in baseball.

Molitor would become many things to the Brewers, a man who worked almost as hard off the field as on. He is almost too thoughtful, too quietly articulate, to be a team leader in the traditional rah-rah sense, but he would lead on the field or use his sense of humor to raise spirits. His leadership abilities would gradually emerge in a variety of other ways as well.

Early in his career, in just his third season, he became the team representative to the Major League Baseball Players Association, responsible for team votes, conveying the strategies of the association to the players and the players' views to the association, and giving statements to the local media about association views on strikes, lockouts, free agency, and league policies on drug testing. Molitor's ability to separate his personal feelings from the players' interests was apparent in the way he handled Peter Ueberroth's call for voluntary drug testing in the mid '80s. Although Molitor had spent a good deal of time publicly regretting his own drug involvement and cautioning young people about the hazards, he joined with the association in warning players against the voluntary tests and the infringement of their rights. When wearing his Players Association hat, he was able to separate himself from his own past and give his fellow players the best possible advice that he could in terms of their individual interests in relationship to the league. His own past culpability, or the thought that his position might seem self-serving, didn't stop him from fulfilling his duties as representative. In later years, he would become a member of the association's Bargaining Committee, often devoting time in the off-season to negotiations of the General Agreement.

A devout Christian, Molitor led the organization of clubhouse chapel, a group that would hold prayer meetings before Sunday games and arrange visiting speakers. His religious faith, though hardly trumpeted from the rooftops, was an important part of his life and a part of his life he took to the clubhouse. He has never been one to thank God publicly for divine intervention in the course of a ball game. When he mentions prayers, they're prayers for character rather than luck, for patience rather than a miracle double.

He was also usually the first Brewer to discuss a game with the press, offering intelligent commentary and giving unstinting praise to his teammates. In later years with the club, he would appear weekly on radio station WKLH, to discuss the Brewers and baseball. He worked hard to bring the community and the team closer together in different ways, organizing the Ignitor Team, to allow disadvantaged seniors and youth the opportunity to attend Brewers games, and participating in sports clinics with children.

Always deeply involved in community work, after the retirement of the very active Cecil Cooper, Molitor would lead the team in the area of public service. Cooper had served on the board of Midwest Athletes Against Childhood Cancer, and later Molitor would sit on the same board. It is an area in which he and Linda Molitor have been particularly active.

Through it all, he somehow managed to become neither the clubhouse lawyer, the clubhouse preacher, nor the official spokesman. He was larger than any of the roles that he assumed. He was a hard-working, skillful player who always put his body on the line to make a play, and who always found time to do more. Genuinely grateful for his talent and for the rewards that it has brought him, Molitor has shown his gratitude — by doing as much for his community as he can. His strong family ties have extended to his teammates and the city in which he lives.

Throughout his years of pro ball, he has maintained a special relationship with the University of Minnesota and its baseball program. He has helped with recruiting by calling prospective players, and has actively sought donations for the department of sports injury. In 1990, he gave the university $100,000 to endow a program of baseball scholarships, and since then has participated in fund-raising games between the Gopher alumni and the current team.

Molitor's exceptional commitment to public service in Milwaukee did not go unacknowledged. At team award ceremonies, he often received the Brewers' "Good Guy" award for public service. In November of 1990, the Milwaukee Council on Alcoholism presented him with its annual award for the All Sports Distinguished Athlete of the Year. The activities cited were extensive. He participated in the Boys and Girls Club sports clinics and in the Athletes for Youth Program. He served on the boards of Midwest Athletes Against Childhood Cancer and The Fellowship for Christian Athletes, and he donated time to the Children's Wish Foundation. The awards dinner itself was to raise funds for anti-alcohol programs in the schools. The list is a long one, but it provides only a glimpse at the amount of time Molitor has given to community programs.

RENEWING THE CONTRACT

Following the season of the streaks, there was more elbow surgery, this time arthroscopy. During the winter, Molitor was awarded the American League's Joe Cronin Award for significant achievement and the Hutch Award for the player making the most notable comeback of the year. It was a significant token of how he had struggled to overcome injury. Previous winners included Mickey Mantle and Carl Yastrzemski.

In January of 1988, Molitor signed with the Brewers for two more years, with a guaranteed $1.4 million per season. The contract was heavily laced with incentives for number of games played. He would receive $50,000 if he played in 81 games and $100,000 for each level if he reached 100, 125, and 150 games.

The Brewers knew what Molitor's injuries had cost them in 1987, just as the injuries had cost them in 1981 and 1984. But there was really no incentive the Brewers could offer Molitor to stay healthy. Did the contract hint that he was malingering? That he could somehow stay healthier or play hurt? The contract really didn't say any of these things. His game depended on that single-minded concentration that would always put him at some risk. Molitor was hardly a player who had shied away from playing hurt. He did it all the time. If there was a way that he could contribute to the Brewers on the field, he was there.

The contract was a simple statement of fact. The more games Molitor could play, the better the Brewers' chance of winning. The more the Brewers won, the better the gate receipts would be. It was simply an acknowledgement of the baseball business in Milwaukee.

Molitor arrived early for training camp and started working out at second base. He had played there with good results at the end of the '87 season, and playing second diminished the risks to his arm that he would be taking at third. He was suffering from a shoulder impingement that made throwing difficult. At training camp, though, he suffered a recurrence of the hamstring problem that had bothered him the year before. The hamstring interfered with his lateral movement in the infield, but he could still run. He would play as DH in the Brewers' opening game against the Orioles, a game in which he managed to steal home once again.

When he finally managed to begin playing in the infield, it was back at third base. By that time, however, the All-Star ballots had already been printed and Molitor was listed at second base — that was where he would play in the All-Star Game after being voted in. His first chance to play at second for the Brewers came just three days before.

Throughout the year, Molitor was playing with a series of nagging injuries, including groin pulls, the ongoing hamstring problem, the shoulder impingement, and a badly sprained wrist. He missed a game in July after what he called a "trifecta," three injections for pain in the groin area, wrist, and shoulder. Despite all that, he was still making a major contribution to the team, managing a .312 batting average and 41 stolen bases by year's end. As long as he could play well, he would contribute to the team. The numbers weren't as good as they had been the previous season, but there was no major injury to interfere with his playing.

His ongoing contribution showed in the Brewers' season. In 1988, with Molitor managing to play 154 games, the Brewers had a winning percentage of .537. They finished in third place, but were just one game behind Detroit and two behind Boston. Facing an off-season without major surgery, Molitor would find more time for baseball. In November of 1988, he joined another all-star team to tour Japan as he had done nine years before. This time Molitor was accompanied by his young family.

HIGH SPIRITS

The shoulder impingement was still causing trouble at the 1989 spring training camp, so once again Molitor was having difficulty playing third base. On the last day of training camp, the final roster was announced. Spirits were running high, and a warm-up lap during the daily workout turned into an all-out race. Molitor found himself losing the race to prospect Dave Engle, who had just survived the final cut. Molitor decided to try sliding past Engle to come in first. He took a swipe as he went past, hitting his finger on Engle's foot. The bit of horse-play dislocated the ring finger on Molitor's right hand. Of all his injuries, it would seem the most ridiculous. The finger required surgery, and Molitor was put on the disabled list.

After the operation, Molitor, still in high spirits, went back to camp to play a practical joke on Engle. He cleaned out the newcomer's locker and left a note directing him to see the general manager. Engle, who actually thought the accident with Molitor might have endangered his chances of making the team, assumed he'd been suddenly cut. As he remarked later, "In Milwaukee, it's God, Robin Yount, and Paul Molitor."

A SKYDOME INTERLUDE

One special moment of the '89 campaign came on June 5. Coming off a 12–9 loss in New York, the Brewers were to face the Jays amid great festivities in Toronto. The Jays were finally moving from the decrepit Exhibition Stadium to a long awaited-facility, the recently completed SkyDome. They had just managed 30 runs in a series against Boston that weekend, and the Jays were looking forward to the kind of attention they'd be getting in their new home.

"I'm going to go down as the first 'something' at Sky-Dome," Molitor joked, as the Brewers faced the Jays' Jimmy Key on Toronto's second opening day of the 1989 season. Molitor had rich memories of the old Toronto ballpark, including the day in April of 1981 when he had played there in the coldest game he could remember. After the game, the Brewers had turned up the showers to get them as hot as possible. Then they made a contest of seeing who could stand in them the longest.

The new stadium was designed to get a different kind of attention. A miracle of engineering, it boasted the world's first retractable dome. There were some pessimists who thought that the vast dome might just get stuck in its movement, leaving the city with a perpetually half-open stadium, but time has luckily proven them wrong.

Molitor was the first hitter to come to bat in the Dome and the first player to get a hit, a grounder to left-center that he pushed to a double. A sacrifice bunt by Robin Yount got him to third base, and a grounder to the shortstop by Gary Sheffield brought him home, scoring the first run to be registered in the Dome. Perhaps reluctant to detract from the spectacle of the stadium itself, or sensitive to the feelings of the crowd, Molitor said later, "I tried not to make too much of my first at bat. But to get a hit, I was relieved."

There were other moments to cheer Toronto fans that day — a two-run homer by Fred McGriff in the second and a solo homer by George Bell in the eighth — but that first game belonged to the visitors. The Brewers won 5–3. Somehow Molitor's place in the history of SkyDome would seem kinder in the future to Toronto fans.

AN UNSATISFYING SEASON

Though the 1989 season had gotten off to a bad start with his dislocated finger, Molitor managed to stay free of major injuries and to play in 155 games, more than he'd played in since 1982. It was one year, though, that his continued play didn't make things significantly better for the Brewers. In August he struggled with a serious hitting slump, averaging just .233 for the month. He managed to reverse it in September, but the Brewers were starting to need far more than just the life in Molitor's bat. At one point in the season, Dan Plesac thought the team looked "dead."

The Brewers ended the season at an even .500. Four years after beginning a major rebuilding effort, the team's performance was still sagging. Although Molitor had a batting average of .315, and Robin Yount's was .318, the team average was only .259. In the closing weeks of the season, Molitor had moved from first to third in the batting order to provide some much-needed run production. There were trade rumors that Molitor was going to San Diego.

Both Molitor and Yount were deeply dissatisfied with the way the team was going. The increasing emphasis on youth seemed to Molitor to be the wrong approach. For some reason the team wasn't gelling the way it had in the past: "I'm not blaming it all on the young players," Molitor explained, "but they have power in numbers and sometimes they've gone off in their own direction. Just watching some people go about their jobs makes you wonder sometimes." Molitor could look back affectionately to the kind of balance the team had had a decade before, when he was first coming up. He thought the Brewers should be looking for some more veteran players to strengthen the lineup.

9

Bargaining

In the early months of 1990, Paul Molitor was a very busy man. So was Bud Selig, the owner of the Milwaukee franchise. The collective bargain between the Players Association and management had run out and Selig, who was chairman of the Player Relations Committee, was also leading the owners' negotiating committee in their attempt to arrive at a new contract. Molitor was one of the negotiators on the players' Bargaining Committee as the two sides met in Tampa, Florida, to hammer out the differences.

They were difficult times for baseball. Many would recall the confusion and acrimony of the strike-shortened season of 1981. To avoid repeating that, the owners decided to take a tough stand, locking out the players when talks bogged down in February. It made more sense to disrupt spring training and have the season start late, than to interrupt it in the middle.

The real problem that Selig had taken to the negotiations had gone unresolved. He was concerned about the changing economics of baseball. The rapid escalation of baseball salaries throughout the '80s was creating sharper and sharper divisions between the haves and have-nots, between the rich teams in major markets with crowded stands and lucrative supplemental television agreements and teams in smaller markets without full bleachers.

Selig was calling for something he called "revenue participation," a way whereby teams could establish a fixed percentage of gross income for players' salaries. He thought the collective bargaining talks were the place to bring it up, but there was no consensus among the owners themselves and it was never dealt with in any substantive way. Molitor, as a spokesman for the players, had already declared in January that he didn't believe "the wolf was at the door" for some of the small-market franchises.

During the same period, Molitor was involved in renegotiating his own contract with the Brewers. The main participants in the talks were the Brewers' general manager Harry Dalton and Molitor's agent, Ron Simon. Talks were not proceeding well, and Molitor had taken the step of applying for arbitration. Robin Yount had already come to terms with the Brewers, but there were unexpected delays in Yount's contract. Yount apparently hadn't signed it and, as a result, it hadn't been filed with the commissioner's office. If the contract had been agreed upon, Simon thought that he and Molitor should have a look at it before coming to terms with the Brewers, but the Brewers simply insisted that the contract wasn't available.

In arbitration, the player and the team each present a figure for the player's services, and the arbitrator picks the figure deemed most appropriate to the player's value. The Molitor/Simon figure was more than Robin Yount had apparently signed for. That hardly seems like an issue, whatever the relative value of the two players, since in some ways a figure is still just a negotiating tool until it goes to binding arbitration. But that year in Milwaukee, baseball salaries were very big news. Molitor eventually had to explain at some length that he wasn't comparing himself to Yount, nor was he saying that he thought he was worth more than Yount. The two men had been close for many years, and it wasn't a debate that Molitor was enjoying.

When it was revealed that both players had signed contracts averaging about $3 million per season, there were protests about the salaries in the Milwaukee papers. There were better teams, in richer markets, that hadn't found it necessary to have two $3 million players on their rosters. Ticket price increases, the inevitable result of escalating salaries, were bad for business. So were highly paid players who couldn't produce. Bud Selig had been privately voicing complaints about both Molitor and Yount for a lack of leadership, but the charge was fair to neither of two fine players who had always led by example.

Molitor had almost always dealt openly with the press, knowing it to be the best policy. Essentially a private person, he was no fonder than anyone else of unpleasant confrontations. When his name had surfaced in the 1984 drug trial, his first response to reporters' queries had been to say nothing. Now he was being embarrassed in a different way. He was open to suspicions that he was a greedy egomaniac without regard for his team. The reality was that, increasingly, the Brewers couldn't compete financially. They have been described in more recent times as the most leveraged team in baseball, a franchise that must inevitably move or be sold.

The longevity of the Milwaukee relationship, despite its stresses, was a tribute to Bud Selig, long one of the most popular owners in baseball, a man who struggled throughout the '80s and early '90s to build and hold together a truly competitive team in an increasingly difficult financial climate. Selig has been described as a fan, rather than an owner. The problem for him was that he had to struggle to get salary caps and revenue distribution while paying out some very high salaries to try to keep the Brewers competitive. It anticipated what would happen the next time contract talks between Molitor and the Brewers came up.

DÉJÀ VU

On the first day of 1990 spring training, Molitor required an injection for what was thought to be tendinitis in his right shoulder. Then on April 1, Molitor had another freak accident in training camp. As he slid headfirst into second base, his right hand went under the bag and he suffered a fracture at the base of his thumb. It was almost exactly a year since he had dislocated his finger in another training-camp accident. It seemed like déjà vu. Molitor was frustrated at the thought of another bad beginning to a season, and he left Compadre Stadium refusing to comment to reporters. He would not return until April 27. When he did, he was playing first base, largely because of the condition of his shoulder, which made play at third impossible.

Then, on June 17, in a road game against Cleveland, Molitor suffered another, more serious, break. When he bunted in the ninth inning, the Cleveland pitcher fielded the ball and threw wide to the first baseman, who was forced to reach into the baseline. As he did so, his glove caught Molitor's hand, breaking the lower knuckle of the left index finger.

This was the most serious of the finger breaks so far. The surgery performed by Paul Jacobs, team physician to the Brewers, required the insertion of a pin into the knuckle. Molitor would be out of the lineup for six to eight weeks. His frustration at the string of injuries was increasingly apparent: "Once again, we find something very strange, very peculiar. Something that doesn't happen very often and I happen to be involved."

When Molitor returned to the lineup at the end of July, the

Brewers were struggling. As usual, he did what he could to raise the play of an organization that was becoming steadily more frustrated and disunited — he hit. In August he enjoyed a minor hitting streak, managing to run it to 19 games from August 6 to August 26. It ended on the same date as the 39-game streak had ended three years before. During the streak his average was .351, better than it had been at any other point in the season. "It wasn't a real pretty streak. I had some 1-for-4s in there. I didn't swing the bat great every game." As with the injuries, so with the streaks. The 1990 streak matched the 19-game streak of 1989. Molitor's seasons seemed to be developing an unpleasant sameness, injuries and streaks falling neatly into slots on the calendar.

The chronic shoulder problem made play at third base impossible, and it was hurting his hitting as well. In his last 17 games in 1990, Molitor was hitting only .191, lowering his average in the injury-shortened season to .285. On September 26, 1990, as the pennant race in the AL East ground down, the Brewers faced the Jays in Milwaukee. Molitor led off for the Brewers in the first inning and hit a home run off David Wells. It was the 27th time Molitor had started a ball game that way — and it would turn out to be a good way to finish the season. In the third inning, Molitor, playing first base, and Jim Gantner, playing second, collided as they both tried to catch a looping hit behind first base. Molitor stayed in the game until the eighth inning, managing to get another base hit, but his right arm was swollen and discolored. It was first described as a strain and the Brewers expected him to miss a game against Chicago, but it turned out to be more serious.

Two days later Molitor faced two separate surgeries. With the kind of grim humor that he'd developed during his injury-plagued career, Molitor called it a "doubleheader." The operation for an impingement in his right shoulder had been scheduled for the day after the season ended, and now there would be another one as well, for the partially torn muscle in his right forearm suffered in the collision with Gantner. The Brewers' physician, Paul Jacobs, used arthroscopy to shave the shoulder blade, freeing the impingement, and to trim down some fraying in the shoulder socket lining. An incision was required to make sure the injury had been repaired completely. In a separate operation, another physician, Dennis Sullivan, repaired the torn muscle.

Only a few games remained in what had been a bad season for the Brewers, so the operations wouldn't mean missing crucial games. The rehabilitation process, however, would be a long one. The forearm would normally have meant a month's recovery, but that hardly counted now. The shoulder would require six weeks' rest, the first three of those with the arm in a plaster splint, and rehabilitation time could be from four to five months. The prognosis was good, and Molitor was expected to be ready for spring training camp. What would be left of his ability to throw a baseball couldn't be predicted.

STRAINED RELATIONS

Nineteen-ninety was a difficult and frustrating year for Molitor. As he faced a fall and winter of rehabilitation, unsure of his playing future, the season left him little to look back on positively. Contract talks had been unpleasant, straining relationships with management. The team hadn't played consistently well. There were new kinds of friction creeping into relationships he had counted on in the past. The Brewers' constant rebuilding wasn't leading to improvement, and younger players on the team often played with a self-serving attitude that Molitor himself had never adopted. Over the Brewers' clubhouse door, there had long been written one word: "Attitude." It didn't mean this one.

Whenever there was dissatisfaction on the team, it was immediately voiced in the press. If management made a move to try to improve play, the new Brewers were concerned only with how it might affect their careers. When Molitor's finger had healed and he was preparing to come off the disabled list at the end of July, it seemed likely he'd be returning to first base. Greg Brock, who'd been the team's first baseman since Molitor's latest injury, wasn't pleased. Even before Molitor had actually returned or gotten medical clearance to play defense, Brock was demanding he be traded if he wasn't going to be the regular first baseman.

Later, Gary Sheffield would suffer from a mysterious ailment and go AWOL, cleaning out his locker and departing for the season without informing the manager. Part of the problem revolved around Sheffield wanting to play shortstop and the Brewers expecting him to play third. Acquiring shortstops and then moving them somewhere else was part of Brewer history. It was the mobility factor. A shortstop needed high mobility and the Brewers would move them around. Gorman Thomas, Yount, Molitor, Dale Sveum, and Sheffield had all played shortstop at one time or another. Only Yount had been allowed to stay at the position until injuries made him an outfielder. Younger players, looking forward to arbitration and free agency, weren't prepared to be flexible.

For Molitor, who had always been flexible, perhaps too flexible, in such matters — he had moved from third to second in 1989 to make room for Sheffield in the infield — the mood of the team was becoming difficult. Relations were strained among players and management, among players and coaches, and among the players themselves. When the players were united, it was against the shortcomings of management, who for years had failed to provide the Brewers with a strength and conditioning coach, an adequate weight room, and an infield instructor. Strained relations detracted from the game, and they also began to affect the way the community related to the team.

From the start of the 1990 season, money had become an increasing concern to Brewers fans. The salaries of Yount, Molitor, and pitcher Ted Higuera were highly publicized, right down to a daily breakdown of what each would lose during the lockout. The lockout had fueled discontent with the salary structure of baseball. There was a good deal of complaining when it was revealed that the Brewers had two players among the ten making $3 million a year. The only other team with two players on the list was the Oakland A's with Dave Stewart and Rickey Henderson. All Oakland had to show for their investment was a World Series victory in 1989 and a third consecutive trip to the World Series at the end of the 1990 season. Milwaukee just got higher ticket prices, a sixth-place team, and newspaper articles that documented players' tantrums and lists of salaries that peaked at $15,000 per day.

Molitor has often spoken about the special bond that existed between him and Yount and Jim Gantner. To Molitor, the long-standing relationship kept them humble in a special way. The relationship and their own personalities may have contributed to that shared attitude, but there were aspects of playing ball in Milwaukee that contributed as well.

Milwaukee is a working-class city, one that prides itself on its work ethic. Built on brewing and industry, it is surrounded by the farmlands and towns of Wisconsin's dairy industry. Fans respond to hard work. It was always one of the qualities about Molitor's play that endeared him to them. Molitor runs out every hit today, as he has run out every hit throughout his career. Whatever his problems off the field, whatever his injuries, Molitor works as hard as any man in baseball.

Milwaukee has never taken to the star system in quite the same way as New York, Oakland, Atlanta, or Toronto. Even Hank Aaron, at the end of his career, didn't get much attention there. Apart from a hard core of fans, only one thing really determines box office in Milwaukee — that's winning. People go to see the team win. If stars help make that possible, that's fine, but it's the winning that counts. The night Molitor's 39-game streak ended was the only time something had mattered more than winning.

The city's appetite for victory might even explain the team's orientation to offense. A good hitter can produce almost every night, while a starting pitcher can only contribute to one game in four. In their best years, the Brewers had had good pitching — Vuckovich, Caldwell, Haas, and later Ted Higuera — but it was always the offense in which the team made the heaviest investment. The one exception was Rollie Fingers, who had contributed so much to Oakland's World Series teams before eventually going to the Brewers, but Fingers had been a closer, and a closer can contribute to almost every game. It was offense that had made the Brewers great in the late '70s and early '80s, and it was pitching that had often kept them from the post-season. Their patchwork defense was another sign of their orientation. When it came to investing in winning, the Brewers were on a tight budget, and it would usually go to offense.

I O

Shifting Positions

The problems of the 1990 season wouldn't go away for the Brewers, but in the next two years the team would show signs of real improvement. Molitor's shoulder surgery of 1990 had effectively ended his career at third and second base, as well as at most of the other positions he'd played for the Brewers. He could play first base effectively, but not on a regular basis. As a result, he found himself increasingly cast in the role of designated hitter. During the 1991 season, he played 46 games at first base and 112 as designated hitter. He had long resisted the duties of the DH. He felt he was in the game more when he was playing in the infield, but the DH role allowed him to play in every game, and it cut down the chance of further injury. While many players have seen the position as the beginning of the end, Molitor didn't take it that way. In the same spirit that he'd played seven other positions for the Brewers, he almost treated it as the beginning of something else. He took it as an opportunity to stay in the lineup, and he worked harder than ever at his hitting.

The result was one of the best seasons of his career. His early season hitting in 1991 was strong enough to lead to his selection to the All-Star team. As before, it was hard to keep track of his position shifts, and consequently he played third base at that year's game. Molitor maintained his momentum throughout the season and finished with a career high of 216 hits, leading the majors by six. He scored 133 runs, 18 more than second place Jose Canseco, and he tied with the White Sox' Lance Johnson to lead the league in triples.

His increasing use as designated hitter seemed to be cutting down on injuries. Not only was it affecting the number of games he could play — he managed to play 158 games, the most he'd played since 1982, and led the majors with 665 at bats — but it also meant that he wasn't playing through the kinds of injuries he had incurred in the field, particularly the hamstring problems.

MAKING CHANGES

The 1992 season began with major changes in the Brewers' staff. Harry Dalton, the man who had become general manager in the same year that Molitor came to the team, was gone, and so too was manager Tom Trebelhorn. Dalton was replaced by Sal Bando and Trebelhorn by Phil Garner. The problematic Gary Sheffield, the Brewers' perennial hope of the future, was traded to San Diego, where he promptly became a star. Garner was finding a new style for the team, emphasizing quality pitching, contact hitting, and baserunning. The mix of veterans and younger players was finally starting to work.

Molitor moved down in the batting order, from lead-off to third. The Brewers had tried the move in the past without success, but now it finally started to work. If batting first had made some good use of Molitor's running game, it failed to exploit his hitting consistency to the limit. This became increasingly true in the late '80s and into the early '90s, when the Brewers lacked the kind of hitters who could be counted on to get Molitor home. There had been times in 1991 when Molitor, never especially feared as a home-run hitter, would be among the most productive Brewers in this category. After switching Molitor in the batting order, the Brewers really started to compete for the lead in the American League East. As much as Molitor had always liked the leadoff spot, there are many who thought the Brewers should have made the move long before.

What really made the difference was that the Brewers were developing players who could play the same game as Molitor but on younger legs. Outfielder Darryl Hamilton, in his fourth season with the team, had tremendous speed on the base paths. He would end the season with a .298 batting average and 41 stolen bases. Rookie shortstop Pat Listach, a late call-up from the minors, took over Molitor's spot at the top of the lineup. Listach, a baserunner with tremendous instincts, turned to Molitor for instruction. The veteran was giving Listach as much advice about the leadoff spot as he could, and he had a pupil worthy of the assistance. By year's end Listach would steal 54 bases, the second highest total in the American League, and post a batting average of .290, a performance that garnered him Rookie of the Year honors.

The pitching staff was also much improved, combining with a new emphasis on defense to produce some of the best numbers in the Brewers' history. Chris Bosio and Jaime Navarro had very good seasons, and there was a brilliant rookie performance: after starting the season in the minors, Cal Eldred won 11 games, while losing just 2. Closer Doug Henry, in just his second season in the majors, got 29 saves. Together they combined for a team ERA of just 3.43, the best record in the American League.

As the new Brewers, long awaited, finally began to arrive, there were fine performances from the trio of players who had been together on the team since 1978. On August 14, Jim

Gantner hit his only home run of the year, but he did it in the thirteenth inning to end a game against the Red Sox. September of 1992 was a heady time for baseball in Milwaukee. Attendance suddenly soared as the team stayed in the race for the American League East and Robin Yount approached his 3,000th hit. It came on September 9.

The Brewers spent the 1992 season in close pursuit of the Toronto Blue Jays for the American League East — unsuccessfully as it would turn out. At the end of the 1992 season, the Brewers were just four games back of the Blue Jays in the division and had the fifth best record in baseball. It just wasn't quite good enough. They failed to advance to the post season for the tenth straight year. As Molitor would later remark, just as the Brewers were getting close, the Blue Jays would pull away.

The move to third in the order demonstrated the effect Molitor's hitting could have on run production — he concluded the year with a career high of 89 RBIS. The focus on his bat, too, was showing. He was overcoming a long-standing reputation as someone who would swing at first pitches, and somehow, at 36, his hitting was getting better. His batting average for May and June was .360 and he ended the season with a .320 average.

The most important thing to happen to Molitor in 1991 and '92 was that he stayed healthy. In 1992, he again managed to play 158 games, and the full year in action, combined with the shift in the batting order, helped the team become contenders.

It's fair to say that, for the decade from 1983 to 1992, as Molitor went so went the Brewers. Tracking his lengthy stints on the disabled list can provide a clear graph of his contribution, as such a method can for almost no other player in the majors. By the end of the 1990 season, he had missed over 500 games during his major league career. What he meant to the team became clear during the streaks of 1987, and it remained clear in the years that followed. In 1989, he played 155 games. The Brewers were .500, eight games back in fourth place, not a bad showing for a team that had injuries, a lack of cohesiveness, and only two really productive hitters. In 1990, the year of the broken fingers and the dysfunctional shoulder, Molitor played in only 103 games, and his batting average fell to .285. The Brewers were suddenly in sixth place, at .457, 14 games back. If Molitor could play a full season, the Brewers were competitive, or could at least play .500 ball. When he shifted to the designated hitter spot as his usual position, the team performance got better. In 1991, he played in 158 games and the Brewers were in fourth place, at .512, eight games back. In 1992, with the best team the Brewers had fielded in a decade, he again played in 158 games and the Brewers finished in second place at .568, four games back.

DIFFICULT CHOICES

As he often had before, Molitor filed for free agency in October of 1992. This time, though, things would be different. In the past, he and the Brewers would file for arbitration and come to terms before the arbitration deadline was reached. Now Molitor and the Brewers were far apart in terms of money and years, and the Brewers were showing no interest in allowing the matter to go to arbitration. Molitor had earned around $3.4 million, with incentives, in 1992. The best that Milwaukee was able to offer for the '93 season was a pay cut of nearly a million dollars. There was a sense that the team simply wasn't interested in signing him, that they couldn't let an arbitrator pick Molitor and Ron Simon's estimate of his value.

In 1992 the Brewers had been seriously competitive, but they had spent $30 million on players' salaries to do it, in what might be baseball's smallest market. Other small-market teams, like the Montreal Expos, were spending half as much. In the four years from 1988 to 1992, the Brewers' player payroll had more than tripled. It was becoming impossible for the smaller-market teams to compete in the new economy of baseball.

The Brewers had signed huge and unproductive contracts with Ted Higuera and Franklin Stubbs, for $13 million and $6 million respectively. Molitor had used the phrase "Pretzel Logic," the title of a Steely Dan song from 1974, to describe some management decisions. They were mistakes the Brewers couldn't afford to make. Higuera's injuries had made his contract particularly unfortunate — the Brewers had finally gambled big on pitching only to see millions go down the drain. The Brewers were not just reluctant to sign another senior player with a history of injuries — they simply couldn't afford to. What they really needed were wise and small investments in young players. They were finally seeing some production from their recent draft picks, something they hadn't seen since they'd drafted Molitor and Yount in the mid-'70s, a generation before. The team's future was in the hands of players like Listach, Eldred, and Henry. The Brewers couldn't pay fair-market value for Molitor's skills.

Molitor and the Brewers were in an economic trap. The Brewers couldn't compete with the major-market teams for Molitor, and yet the only way the team could generate revenue was by winning baseball games. The records would demonstrate how much Molitor had contributed to the team's better seasons. The most productive of the veterans, he was still making an essential contribution, was still the "Ignitor," but the Brewers were reaching the point where they couldn't afford to compete for Milwaukee fans or the American League East.

Sal Bando was aggressively downscaling Molitor's value in comments to the press. Bando went so far as to describe the DH role as "a part-time job," and added, "The guy who hits home runs and drives in a lot of runs has one value and the guy that does what Paul does has a different value." It was true. It just wasn't true in the way Bando intended it. The Brewers' claims to be trying to sign Molitor seemed largely an exercise in public relations doubletalk: to give the impression that they wanted to keep him while elsewhere diminishing his value in the eyes of fans. Clearly, the time had come for Molitor to seriously consider other offers.

While negotiations stalled in Milwaukee, the Boston Red Sox, the California Angels, and the Toronto Blue Jays were all expressing degrees of interest. In November, when Molitor was in Minneapolis for Kirby Puckett's pool tournament, he joked with Dave Winfield about joining him on the Jays.

Late in the same month, Molitor met over dinner with Pat Gillick, general manager of the Jays, and Paul Beeston, president of the club, in Milwaukee's Sanford Restaurant. Molitor was particularly interested in the executives' assurances that they wanted to repeat as World Series champions in 1993. The post-season was now what mattered most to Molitor in baseball. He had tasted it early in his career, as a 26-year-old, and he had performed well in a losing cause. Toronto represented the chance to play for a winner.

Molitor had devoted his career to the Brewers and to the life of Milwaukee as no other player had. He wanted nothing more than to remain in Milwaukee and play for a championship team. After years in the desert, the 1992 Brewers had finally looked like winners. He was faced with an unusual choice: take a pay cut and a one-year contract to stay with a team that might be competitive, or increase his earnings, get job security, and play for a team that had just managed to become world champions without him. It was no choice at all, however strong his attachments to the organization, the other players, and the city.

While Ron Simon and Sal Bando were still negotiating,

The tearful press conference where Molitor
announces his signing with the Blue Jays.

THE MILWAUKEE JOURNAL

Molitor came to terms with the Blue Jays on December 6 for $13.5 million for three seasons, with an option for a fourth year. Milwaukee had finally offered arbitration, but it was a move that suggested either an attempt to get some compensation from the team that signed Molitor, or more public relations to save face before the home fans. When Pat Gillick announced the signing, he described Molitor as "the best offensive player in the league — without a lot of power."

Saying good-bye to Milwaukee was a difficult experience. Throughout the season, Molitor had appeared weekly on the city's WKLH radio. He went on the show again a day after signing with the Jays. Though there had been many provocative and contradictory statements made in the press, Molitor cut quickly to the economic reality of the situation. "It was evident from the start that [the Brewers] are in a very, very sticky position as far as how fragile this franchise is — and maybe a lot of the small-market franchises. So for the last few days I have been trying to prepare myself for the possibility that it wasn't going to happen."

Molitor always tried to take the high road, and he was even understanding about Bando's comments. "Sal has had a difficult job through this negotiation. I think he was limited in what he could do. I think, when pressed, it became difficult to try to explain it. It became difficult to try to explain it in terms of rationalization of why the Brewers couldn't do what maybe they hoped they could do. I tried not to take anything personally throughout this thing because I do understand his position. It saddens me that it's that way more than anything else."

The way Molitor was able to rationalize Bando's comments was a reflection of the way he had learned to play baseball. He played almost without a self. He would concentrate himself into a pitcher's timing, into his motion, to get himself into an ideal relationship with the ball, whether it was to hit or steal a base. That was where the joy came from, the freedom that arose from getting perfectly synchronized with the action in the field. Molitor's modesty was part of his genius. It allowed him to see the bigger picture, whether he was playing ball or reflecting on comments made during negotiations.

Molitor then talked on the radio about calling Robin Yount to let him know what had happened. Feelings were different, and he couldn't distance himself from the attachment he felt to his friend and the real sorrow he felt at leaving Milwaukee. Molitor's voice was cracking as he described the conversation, and he was unable to continue.

In Milwaukee, there was shock at the signing. The *Milwaukee Journal* ran pages of letters from frustrated fans. Some thought Molitor simply greedy, but most of them directed their anger at the team. Bando's response was to blame the fans: "If all the fans were upset, where were they the last 15 years we had him?"

No one would protest the move more vocally than Robin Yount and Jim Gantner. "I think it stinks," Yount told reporters. "I think it's a sad day when one of the best players in the American League wants to stay in a city with a team he's been a part of for a long time and the organization can't afford to keep him. I'm going to sit down here and weigh out what should be done and how badly I really want to come back, knowing that a lot of the Milwaukee Brewers have left now." For Gantner, facing retirement from the game, it was "a nightmare": "With an individual like Paulie, you know the small markets really are in trouble. If Paul Molitor leaving the Brewers doesn't show that the small markets are in trouble, nothing does."

The 1992 season had begun with the departure of Gary Sheffield. It was ending with the departure of Molitor. What was apparent to Yount, who had always played to win, who had never cared about MVP awards while winning two of them, was that the organization just couldn't afford to pay for winning baseball. Yount and Gantner knew better than any-one else the part that Molitor had played in the Brewers' chemistry.

Molitor's feelings about leaving Milwaukee were very mixed. He had spent 15 seasons in the city, more years than most players can hope to spend in the majors. His playing had made him one of the city's most popular athletes, and his community involvement had made him a bulwark of local charities. He felt like he was being forced out by the pay cut offered. Later, he would say to Bud Selig, "I was a victim of the system, wasn't I?"

Molitor wasn't just moving to another team. He was moving to another country, to a very different country. He was moving to a city where you could get your name in Coca Cola jingles. He was stepping out of what might have been the Original American Closet.

PAUL MOLITOR:
TORONTO BLUE JAY

"That's one good thing about baseball. You always get another chance. In baseball, you get 600 chances a year."

Paul Molitor

11

"The Best Organization in Baseball"

The 1992 Blue Jays were the first team outside the United States to win a World Series, and they did it in their 16th season. During the year, Dave Winfield's relationship with Toronto had become a special one. Until 1992 the Toronto fans had been notorious throughout the American League for sitting on their hands, or else holding those hands over their mouths. They were so reserved that home-field advantage was thought by some to be no advantage at all. It wasn't that Toronto crowds didn't like baseball — on the contrary, they often set attendance records — but they gave little vocal support to their team.

Winfield, perhaps more than anyone else, changed that. The man who had once, as a New York Yankee, been led off the field of Toronto's old Exhibition Stadium by police after managing to kill a seagull with a throw, had become one of the most popular players in the history of the city, an elegant, larger-than-life veteran and future Hall of Fame candidate who seemed to embody the spirit of the game. When Winfield commanded "Dave Wants Noise," the Toronto fans responded, casting aside their notorious reserve and, finally, after 16 years of silence, getting into the spirit of the game. Among Winfield's accomplishments, getting Toronto fans to find their voice ranks high.

It would be an understatement to say that their newfound enthusiasm was rewarded. In 1992, a team that had suffered in the past from every kind of personnel problem imaginable finally learned how to play as a team. Gone were such notoriously quixotic figures as George Bell, a master of colorful language, whether directed at teammates, reporters, or fans, who had once invited fans to "kiss my purple butt."

Free-agent signings of legendary veterans, like Winfield and pitcher Jack Morris, fresh from leading the Minnesota Twins to the 1991 World Series, lent luster to an already excellent roster. Joe Carter was a team leader, both on the field and off. There were standouts, too, among the young: pitcher Juan Guzman, in just his second season in the majors; John Olerud, a gifted hitter and first baseman who had overcome brain surgery at 21 to carve out a career for himself in the majors; and Roberto Alomar, a second baseman who might be the purest baseball talent on the roster.

It was a wonderful team, but not one that could be held together in its entirety for the coming season. One commentator remarked that teams usually had to pay players for a World Series after they had won it, but Toronto had paid in advance. The Blue Jays had to put the brakes on their escalating payroll — at $50 million the highest in baseball.

The pitching staff was the hardest hit. David Cone, a last-minute acquisition from the New York Mets for the pennant drive, went to the Kansas City Royals, not far from his hometown. Jimmy Key, a career Blue Jay and a standout in the World Series after an uneven season beset by injuries, wanted more years on his contract than the Jays could agree to. He went to the New York Yankees. It might have been the worst miscalculation the Jays' front office had made since they'd named the unpopular Jimy Williams as manager in 1986. Tom Henke, "The Terminator," a brilliant closer, left for the Texas Rangers.

Gone too were Candy Maldonado, Kelly Gruber, and Dave Winfield. Though Molitor had joked with Winfield about joining him on the Jays, the reality turned out to be very different. After batting in the winning run in the 11th inning of the final game of the World Series, and after meeting the city's thunderous applause at a victory reception, Winfield found little apparent interest from the team's management in his continuing to play ball in the city. Perhaps thought too old at 41 to figure in the Jays' plans for even another year, Winfield went to the Minnesota Twins on a two-year deal.

THE REINVENTION OF THE BLUE JAYS

The sense of calculation may be what unites the best executives and the best players in baseball. In a game where there is always risk, the best players are those who calculate the odds of success against the price of failure. The mind that must weigh the chances of a multiyear, multimillion-dollar deal for an aging player paying off, in the long run, is very much like the mind that will calculate, in the very short term, the chances of stealing a base or the pitch that might best elude an opposing bat. It is a quality that will unite a Pat Gillick or a Paul Beeston, architects of the Blue Jays' success, with a Paul Molitor or a Jack Morris.

There were many who doubted the Jays management's commitment to winning after the 1992 World Series. They might have the best organization in baseball, but the Jays had long cultivated a reputation for choking. There had been times in the recent past when the Jays had been thought the most talented team in baseball, only to blow out in the final games of the season, or fail to advance from the ALCS.

Given this view, the 1992 season could look like a fluke, managed on single-season and late-season acquisitions. During the World Series, some of the players who had looked best

JEFF GOODE, THE TORONTO STAR

were Cone, Winfield, and Key. The Jays had hardly tried to keep them, while there was even talk that Joe Carter would go to Kansas City. There was a general impression that the Jays organization (read Labatt's, the brewing industry giant that owns 90 percent of the team), by virtue of the World Series win, could justify turning their attention now to the bottom line of profitability.

Despite this, Molitor accepted Gillick and Beeston's real commitment to fielding the best team they could in the hope of repeating the 1992 triumph. The Jays had won the AL East in three of the previous four seasons. They had a habit of winning.

Gillick and Beeston showed the same kind of insight. The Jays had a long-standing policy of offering only short contracts. The reason that Jimmy Key had gone to the New York Yankees was that the Jays weren't interested in the length of contract he was demanding. Manager Cito Gaston, who first joined the Jays' coaching staff in 1981, had spent a long time with the organization before he glimpsed anything resembling job security. Contract length may have been an issue in the failure to sign Winfield. Paul Molitor — who, at 36, was one of the older players in the game and, beyond that, had incurred numerous injuries, some of the kind that had ended other players' careers — hardly seemed like a player that the Jays might gamble on, even in the mid-term.

In times of economic constraint, at a time when the team no longer had anything to prove, the Jays were offering a three-year contract, at $4.5 million a season, to a 36-year-old DH who, they admitted, didn't have a lot of power. Clearly, all three men had seen something in each other that many were missing: a genuine, even absolute, commitment to winning. In 1992 Gillick and Beeston had watched Milwaukee pursue the Jays. They had seen what Molitor had contributed to that effort. They were investing in character and desire, the fuel that drove Molitor's talent. For his part, Molitor had worked as hard as he could all season, pushing himself and the Brewers to their limits, only to see the Jays repeatedly pull away. He had seen his old friend Dave Winfield finally win a World Series, had seen another old friend, Jack Morris, win his second. The possibility of post-season play was in itself a strong incentive, but Molitor's contract also included a bonus of $50,000 should he be World Series MVP. He had always liked his Milwaukee contracts, too, to be rich in incentives. It gave him something to look forward to.

The Jays' wholesale shuffling of personnel in the final weeks of 1992 gave many the impression of a rebuilding year. Some did not expect them to even win the American League East, picking instead the younger and very promising Baltimore Orioles or the New York Yankees to take the division. The Blue Jays, however, were nothing if not still willing to pay for talent. The Milwaukee press had made much of what it called the "three million league" back at the start of the 1990 season. Of the ten players then on the list, none of them had been Blue Jays. Now the Jays were redressing the balance. At the start of the 1993 season, three of those men, Joe Carter, Dave Stewart, and Molitor, were playing for Toronto and a fourth, Rickey Henderson, soon would be. Stewart had been the starting pitcher in the Jays' two losses to Oakland in the 1992 ALCS. He wouldn't be a threat in 1993.

The 1993 Jays would prove to be a very different team than they had been a year earlier. The new season would raise some questions about the fabled astuteness of Beeston and Gillick, the men most responsible for taking the team from struggling expansion franchise to division champions and then to American League champions and on to the World Series. For one thing, the Jays' strength at the mound seemed to be an illusion. The starters struggled or put in time on the disabled list. Morris suffered from injuries and inconsistency, as did Dave Stewart. The Jays were challenged by the Yankees, with Jimmy

Key pushing toward what could be his first twenty-win season. Key was reaching his peak just as Morris and Stewart seemed to be going over the hill. The only pleasant surprise in the Jays' pitching was Pat Hentgen, who posted 19 wins by the end of the season.

If they had misjudged the strength of their pitching, though, they had created one of the greatest offensive threats in baseball's recent history. It's one of the ironies of fan perception that the loss of Dave Winfield was read as part of the Jays' lack of commitment. The shift from Winfield to Molitor was a key to the kind of team the Jays were assembling in the wake of the World Series win.

The talent of the new Jays was less in the home-run department than earlier teams. They no longer had a George Bell who might lead the league in homers while sowing dissension with every breath. Management had shown for some time a willingness to trade big hitters or let them go elsewhere, whether young or old. In recent years they had given up Bell, Fred McGriff, and Cecil Fielder. After the World Series win, they gave up Winfield, Candy Maldonado, and Kelly Gruber. What they sought was speed and consistency, and what they had was one of the quickest teams in history, a team that could ignite the base paths. SkyDome, Toronto's state-of-the-art, retractable domed stadium, would influence team style. In some ways the best of most worlds, it had short fences, very quick turf, and it guaranteed that no one would ever have to hit into a strong wind.

A NEW TEAM, A NEW NUMBER, A NEW HOME

Molitor approached his new club and his new home with a single-minded determination, trying to put behind him the sudden and unexpected departure from Milwaukee. In January

1993 he appeared with a Jays tour group to talk about the team's upcoming season. Then the 36-year-old veteran showed up early at training camp in Dunedin, Florida, getting ready for the season with the team's youngest and least-experienced players. It wasn't something that veteran stars were expected to do, but he'd done it before at the Brewers' spring training camps in Arizona. It impressed his new team and impressed the junior players. If Molitor was prepared to work that hard, maybe they should too.

As the camp developed, Molitor expressed his concern about a lack of focus: "I would like to see some goals implemented. I think we need some intermediate goals. Winning starts with desire, and I think we'll talk about that: what kind of goals we set as a team — to win every series, to win every month, whatever."

Molitor took another step, too, to make himself part of the city he was coming to. He actually moved his family and his permanent residence to Toronto. That wasn't something that would necessarily impress his new teammates, since none of them had taken the step, but it certainly impressed Toronto fans as it became more widely known during the season.

When he had first signed with the Jays, someone in Milwaukee had asked if he would continue to wear the number 4. At the time, he replied, "Is that Canadian or American? Maybe it will turn out to be 3." The number 4 on a Toronto uniform had long been worn by Alfredo Griffin, so Molitor chose the number that had once belonged to Fred McGriff, 19. Molitor wasn't thinking about Fred McGriff, though. He chose the number as an affectionate tribute to Robin Yount.

Trying to fit in with the Jays, Molitor's thoughts were often with his old teammate. After Jim Gantner had had shoulder surgery, effectively ending his career, Yount was left as the only original member of the team Molitor had joined in 1978. Recalling the atmosphere of the Milwaukee clubhouse, Molitor would wonder about how Yount was getting along. "Robin just doesn't know a lot of guys on the team, and I worry about that. I mean, who's he going to eat breakfast with on the road?"

Molitor got off to a very spotty start with the Jays, and the team was unimpressive at the season's beginning. In his first 20 at bats in his new uniform, Molitor managed only three hits. After 33 games, the Jays were 16–17, a game below .500. He sometimes hoped that it hadn't been simply greed that had sent him from the Brewers to the Jays.

It was hard at times for Molitor to find his role with the new team. When Ed Sprague and Turner Ward turned to him for leadership, encouraging him to talk to the rest of the flagging team, Molitor was surprised. He still saw himself as the "new guy." He had come from a team where leadership had always come from the "old guys," where he and Yount and Gantner had spent fifteen years together. Furthermore, he had always led by example rather than speeches. Sometimes anxious about taking the place of Winfield, Molitor was reassured by Joe Carter, who told him to "just be yourself. We know how good you are." It was sound advice, and Molitor found himself gradually getting accustomed to the first new uniform he'd worn in 15 years.

In May, when the team's performance was uneven, Molitor hit .370 and was named American League Player of the Month. Frequently platooned at first base with John Olerud, Molitor began to be an important influence on the young hitter.

12

Home and Away

Molitor's first series against his former teammates was in the SkyDome, and the Jays and Brewers split the four games evenly. During the series, Yount and Molitor seemed to vie for who could be the most valuable player in the park, just as they had once done for the same team. By the time the series ended, Molitor had 7 hits in 15 trips to the plate, while Yount had 8 for 15. Over the last two games, Yount had seven consecutive hits. Yount would say he wasn't usually that streaky, but clearly playing on the same field with his friend had let him briefly find his old form. It gave a sense of the competitiveness that had always fueled their production in Milwaukee. Getting into the spirit of playing for a rich team, Molitor joked: "Maybe Robin'll be the player we'll pick up along the way this year." The season was only a couple of months old, and Molitor was already thinking like a Blue Jay.

His return to Milwaukee on June 25 was more emotional. While one detractor displayed a "Welcome Back Judas" banner just above the Jays' dugout and another carried a sign reading "Season's Greedings," the crowd of over 39,000 was overwhelmingly supportive. Molitor's homecoming was advertised on the radio for a week before the Jays appeared. The number of fans was more than double the usual attendance at County Stadium, more than had turned out for the 36th game of the 1987 hitting streak. Even as a Jay, Molitor was helping the Brewers financially. He received a standing ovation when he first appeared at the plate. The loyalty of the Milwaukee fans was very moving. There was little animosity left for Molitor among the few who had ever felt it, and little animosity left for the organization that had let him go. The departure had been an expression of the mysterious and irresistible forces of the marketplace. Now there was just a sense of loss and some joy at seeing what they had once had. Milwaukee's biggest celebrations had had to come in defeat: the loss to the Cardinals in 1982, and the hitting streak of 1987 that could only be celebrated when it ended.

Molitor rose to the attention the way he always had, showing the powers of concentration he had when he was expected to perform. When his single scored Devon White to give the Blue Jays a 1–0 lead over the home team, he received another standing ovation. The other Jays were impressed by Milwaukee fans as well as by Molitor.

MOVES AT MIDSEASON

Molitor and Dave Stewart didn't have much time to feel like the new guys. The midseason acquisitions were along soon: Tony Fernandez came back as shortstop from the Mets after Dick Schofield broke his arm, and then Rickey Henderson was acquired from the A's. The Jays' absolute devotion to contact hitting and baserunning was confirmed by the new arrivals. Fernandez still held the Jays' record for batting average, and it was only a year since baseball managers had picked Henderson and Molitor as the best base runners in the game.

The midseason acquisitions also threatened to bring back problems the Jays had seemed to have outgrown. Fernandez, if brilliant at shortstop and sometimes brilliant at bat, could still be moody, whimsical, and inconsistent. Traded with Fred McGriff to the San Diego Padres in 1990 for Joe Carter and Roberto Alomar, Fernandez had been languishing with the New York Mets. The acquisition of Rickey Henderson, acknowledged king of the stolen base, hinted at the ego-driven Jays of old. Henderson's acquisition, however, might have been merely symbolic. If in the balance of the 1993 season he seldom showed the spark that had burned the Jays when he played for Oakland, there remained Alomar, Molitor, and White to reveal the same base-stealing skill.

When Henderson joined the Jays, whose roster already had a surplus of contact hitters and base runners, there was immediate questioning about what shape the batting order would take. Tony Fernandez had been batting leadoff for the Mets, Henderson had earned his reputation as the best leadoff man in baseball, and Devon White had been striking out too often in the early part of the season. Cito Gaston asked each of the Jays' first five hitters to make up a batting roster for the team. To Molitor's surprise, when the new order emerged, Gaston had him hitting sixth, following Henderson, White, Alomar, Carter, and Olerud. Molitor and Alomar would switch positions in the order against left-handed pitching. Later Molitor would commend the decision, saying it showed confidence in Devon White and encouraged the recovery his hitting was to show during the season.

But it was a strange order, and one that would receive comment throughout the season. After all, Molitor had only moved from first to third in the Brewers' order early in the '92 campaign. What it depended on was Molitor showing some power to get runners home, and Fernandez, Sprague, and Pat Borders showing some inspired hitting to benefit Molitor on the base paths. There was a chance of squandering Molitor's gift of getting on base. One critic thought it was folly to have

Olerud and Molitor, the leading hitters in the American League, batting fourth and sixth. The Jays might have been better with Olerud and Molitor moved up in the lineup, but the argument was probably meaningless. The Jays' lineup was so rich in hitting and baserunning that constant tinkering with the batting order might not make a difference.

BALTIMORE: THE 1993 ALL-STAR GAME

The Jays' image in baseball was front and center at the 1993 All-Star Game. Cito Gaston, manager of the American League side by reason of the World Series victory, was accused of loading the team with Blue Jays personnel. In all, seven Blue Jays went to the game: Olerud, Alomar, and Carter were voted to the team, while Gaston had chosen Molitor, Devon White, Duane Ward, and Pat Hentgen.

Although Gaston, notoriously loyal to his players, might have gotten slightly carried away, none of the choices was inappropriate. In some sense his actions were quite fitting, since the Blue Jays were coming to look increasingly like an all-star team. They were a very rich club that consistently reinvested in the quality of their product. In the largest American markets — New York, Chicago, San Francisco, and Los Angeles — fan support was divided between American and National League franchises, while the Blue Jays enjoyed almost a national fan base and benefited from national television contracts.

The peak of fan dissatisfaction came when Baltimore pitcher Mike Mussina began warming up in the eighth inning. The warm-up was entirely Mussina's idea, but it later appeared as if Gaston were warming up a Baltimore pitcher he had no intention of using. The Baltimore fans were

The Blue Jay All-Star contingent.

J. MAHLER, THE TORONTO STAR

incensed, taking the situation as a direct insult to their team and an abuse of their players.

Their feelings may have been partly justified. By the eighth inning, the score was so lopsided in favor of the American League side that Gaston could have inserted anyone just to please the fans in the host city. But he didn't. Gaston's parting comment would further rile Baltimore. Gaston said of Mussina, "I just won't take him next year." The remark was loaded. Gaston, at the halfway mark in the season, fully expected to be managing next year's American League All-Star team by going back to the World Series. There would be a new edge to future meetings between the two clubs.

The All-Star Game would help cement the team, at the same time that it became a focus for hostility around the league. Molitor had been on five All-Star teams before, and it was a change to be going with six teammates instead of going as his team's sole representative, as he had for the past two years. The Jays' display might smack of arrogance, but it was a refreshing position for Molitor to be in.

There had been seasons when Molitor had struggled to carry the Brewers to a level they couldn't reach. There'd been other struggles in recent years, when he and Yount and Gantner had suffered with injuries and the mood in the clubhouse had grown more divisive. There were times during the 1993 season when the Jays would struggle, but there was such an abundance of talent that it would never fall to Molitor alone to raise the team. The Jays were used to winning. Many had World Series rings from 1992, and Stewart and Henderson had them from 1989. Molitor didn't have to show what it took to win, even if he had a single-minded drive toward that ultimate goal. He was quiet and self-contained, but he brought an intense determination to every game. He could kindle the drive that was waiting there in the others, and when his teammates discussed the player who contributed most to the team, it was Molitor's name that would emerge. Dave Stewart offered the highest compliment, saying he had always thought the A's' Carney Lansford was the best team player in baseball, but Molitor had made him change his assessment.

Molitor became increasingly comfortable with the team as the season went along. There were other veterans on the team whom he'd long admired from the opposing dugout, players like Morris, Stewart, Carter, and White. He felt a difference, too, between the attitude of some of the Jays' younger players and the attitude that had too often been present on some of the recent Brewers' teams. John Olerud had been shifted from first base to make room for Dave Winfield in the outfield during the 1992 World Series, and now he sometimes shared duties at first base with Molitor. Ed Sprague, too, had been shuffled around, going from backup catcher to third base at the start of the season. They did it without complaining.

Molitor was forming strong bonds with these younger players. He had a wealth of experience in the infield and at the plate, and he was happy to share it. A poll of coaches would choose Molitor as the possessor of the best "smarts in a baseball sense" in the game. He had the most acute observations of pitchers available. He had learned from every player and manager and hitting instructor he'd encountered, and hitting instruction was an area in which the Brewers had never stinted. During Molitor's years in Milwaukee, the hitting instructors had included Frank Howard and Don Baylor.

Throughout much of the season, John Olerud was the focus of attention. The 24-year-old first baseman was maintaining a .400 batting average through July and into August. He had a fine hitting streak going too, eventually running it to 26 games for a team record. Olerud, who had started with the Jays as a designated hitter before becoming the regular first baseman, is a rare talent, gifted with a wonderful, easy swing that seems almost casual but has devastating results. It was a marked contrast to Molitor's sudden and explosive approach to the ball.

Olerud is a remarkably relaxed player, but as the season wore on, Molitor's experience would tell. He is at his best in clutch situations and stretch drives. At the end of the season, Olerud's average would fall to .363, still the best in the majors. Molitor, with more experience, would end the season in second place with .332, but his average after the All-Star break, the midpoint in the season when the division races with New York and Baltimore started to heat up, was .361. He thrives on tough situations, and his durability and determination were now showing. He was pacing the season.

13

The Stretch Drive

September began ominously with the team suddenly spiraling into a six-game losing streak during a road trip against some of the weakest teams in the American League West. It should not have happened. The Jays had been better on the road than division rivals during the season. At the end of the slide, on September 10, they found themselves tied with the Yankees in first place, with the Orioles just half a game back. They would end the season with a four-game visit to Baltimore and it would not be a series for the faint of heart. The Orioles had played well against the Jays all season, and spirits would be running high in Baltimore, where fans were still outraged by their perceptions of the All-Star Game.

On September 15, 1993, in one of the longest nine inning baseball games on record, Paul Molitor batted in his 100th RBI of the season for the first time in his career. Not only was he setting a personal record, but Molitor was also the first player in history ever to reach that plateau for the first time at age 37. What made Molitor's achievement possible was that it was perhaps the first time he'd been on a team that gave him the opportunity to do it. Batting further down in the order was a contributing factor, but Molitor had batted third in 1992. He was benefiting from the other Blue Jays' ability to get on base, just as they were benefiting from the range of skills he could bring to the plate with men in scoring position. The strategic gifts of a Paul Molitor shine brightest on a team that is in contention.

The 1993 Blue Jays were the perfect team for Molitor, because it was a team that was strongest in his area of specialization: consistent and strategic hitting and brilliant baserunning. Once called the best base runner in baseball, his talent barely stood out on the Jays, where the very fast Henderson, Alomar, and White were constants and the backups included the still very quick Alfredo Griffin as a pinch runner. Opposition teams couldn't pitch around anyone on the Jays. The bottom end of the lineup included Ed Sprague, who only a year before had hit a game-winning homer in the World Series and catcher Pat Borders, whose batting average had made him World Series MVP in 1992. Similarly, opponents often couldn't focus on a single base runner if two or more of them managed to get on base.

Molitor was concerned with keeping his focus on the end of the season, and he worried about the team assuming too much because of its lineup. "I don't think we've played well enough to be complacent," he told a reporter. "It's not that we've ever taken anything for granted, but there have probably been days when we've come out thinking things were going to happen simply because of the talent we have. Sometimes it doesn't, but I like to think that's more a matter of us not getting it done because we've tried to do too much. Right now, we have to focus on what it is we have to do." Molitor was taking nothing for granted. He was doing everything he could to be ready. Even late in September Molitor would still take early batting practice following an off-day. He was concerned with maintaining his form, keeping his head straight, not jerking his shoulder up — the things that could creep into his swing.

On September 21, the Jays began a three-game home series against Boston. On the same day, Jack Morris had torn ligaments diagnosed in his elbow. He would be gone for the season, and there was instantly talk of the Jays buying out his contract for the '94 season. It was a terrible day for veterans. Elsewhere, Nolan Ryan, 46 years old and in his 27th year in the majors, was pulled from a game in the third inning. Molitor had long wanted to play on a team with Morris, and he felt Morris's absence particularly. A sudden change of fortune could happen so easily to a veteran, and Molitor's awareness of that potential was one of the things that drove him in his every at bat.

Todd Stottlemyre was to pitch against the Red Sox' Roger Clemens in the first game, and they were not pitchers one would normally pick for a duel. Stottlemyre, dogged throughout his career by control problems, both for his pitches and his temper, was at best inconsistent. He was thought by many at this point in the season to be en route to the bullpen from the starting rotation. Stottlemyre might be impressive if he could just stay in the game.

The game was tight until the fourth inning, when Molitor managed to get to second. Joe Carter, who had not been hitting well even as the Jays had built an eight-game winning streak, managed to connect for a double, bringing Molitor home. It would be the only run the Jays needed.

Given the lead, Stottlemyre pitched the finest game of his career, going on to a complete-game shutout with just three hits and a career-high 13 strikeouts. The Jays had come back from the losing streak that began the month to tie a club record for nine consecutive wins.

Interviewed after the game, Paul Molitor's smile played around the edges of his mouth. "We've talked about it for months. If we could get some good hitting and some good pitching at the same time we could take off." It looked like they might be coming together at just the right time. The immediate competition obliged by going on losing streaks of their own. With only a dozen games left, the Yankees were suddenly five games back and the Orioles five and a half.

For Molitor the season was coming together as it never had before. When he played for the Brewers in 1982, the division had only been decided in the final game of the season. In other years, in 1987 and 1992, the season had ended in desperate races against all probability. Finally, a division race might be turning into a walk. The Jays were in control.

The next night, once more against Boston, Molitor had his 200th hit of the 1993 season. It was the third time he'd reached that plateau, and it was the first time a member of the Jays had passed the 200-hit mark in a season since Tony Fernandez set the club record of 213 during the 1986 season. In fact, it was only the second time a Blue Jay had surpassed 200 hits in a season. As SkyDome erupted with a standing ovation, Molitor touched the brim of his batting helmet in the most modest of acknowledgements.

Characteristically, even though Molitor was leading the league in hits, he was more concerned with the outcome of the game than with his personal achievement. After the overtime loss to Boston ended the team's winning streak at nine games, he told the *Toronto Star*'s Allan Ryan, "I didn't expect we'd win the last 20 in a row. It was a heckuva run at a critical time for us. We battled away, but it's still disappointing to lose, especially knowing the two closest teams had also lost. The thing is, you want to get as free as you can. Put it away — the sooner the better." Of the Yankee loss, he commented, "They didn't take advantage of it when we were struggling and I think they might be feeling that was their chance. Us getting hot right after that might have knocked the wind out of their sails."

Later, though, Molitor would reveal how much the 200th hit had meant to him and the standing ovation that had gone with it. It was the moment at which he felt fully that he was "Paul Molitor — Blue Jay."

YANKEES AT SKYDOME, SEPTEMBER 24–26

The chance to "put it away" was coming in a three-game series against the Yankees. Sweep the Yankees, technically five and a half games back, and the Blue Jays would eliminate the threat from New York.

The Yankees came into SkyDome nursing a wounded team and a chance at winning the American League East that was little more than a numerical possibility. The Jays had ten games left, the Yankees eight. The Jays' "magic number," the number of Jays wins and Yankee losses needed to clinch the division, was down to five. Each game against the Yankees was worth two.

But the Jays had batted badly all season against left-handers and the Yankees were starting left-handers in all three games. They would begin by putting their best arm forward: Jimmy Key, a contender for the Cy Young Award with a record of 17 wins and 5 losses. Key had won both times in two previous encounters against his former teammates. There was talk of the Jays' 1987 season when they had enjoyed a similar lead, only to watch it evaporate and Detroit take the division title. The loss of Key might come back to haunt the Jays' fans and management alike.

The special drama of baseball consists in the isolation of the pitcher — that, and the isolation, too, of the batter. The drama was particularly acute as Key started against his former team. He had been perhaps the most brilliant of the Jays' pitchers during the 1992 World Series: dropped from the starting rotation for the ALCS, he had come back in the series to start and win the fourth game and to win the sixth game in relief. The

D. LOEK, THE TORONTO STAR

Yankee catcher, Mike Stanley, was playing with an injured right hand. During the early innings, he kept getting hit by tipped foul balls, and there were frequent interruptions as Yankee personnel came on the field to check the hand.

The game seemed to bear as much on the past as it did on the future, as old confrontations and allegiances were being recast. The Oakland A's had beaten Toronto for the American League in 1989 and had gone on to win the World Series. As a member of the Oakland A's, Rickey Henderson had seemed to own Jimmy Key. Now, with their affiliations changed, Henderson was the first Jay Key was to face. It would tell much about what the Jays had given up and what they had gained.

In the Jays' first at bat, Henderson hit Key for a double. Next up, Devon White singled, advancing Henderson to third. Paul Molitor, batting third against a left-hander, hit a sacrifice fly to right field, bringing Henderson home for the game's first run. Leading off again in the third, Henderson connected with Key's first pitch for a home run.

Old allegiances would prove just as telling. Jays catcher Pat Borders, MVP in the '92 World Series, knew Key's pitching better than any other player in the game. In his first at bat, in the second inning, Key struck Borders out, making it look easy. But in the fourth, Borders caught a Key pitch for a single, driving in runs by Olerud and Alomar.

By the end of the game, Henderson had crossed home plate three times, single-handedly equalling the run production of the Yankee team. The final score was 7 to 3. Pat Borders had driven in the winning run. The Yankees were six and a half games back and the Jays' number had suddenly dropped to three against the Yankees. Meanwhile, Baltimore obliged by losing to Detroit, leaving the Orioles seven games back and making the Jays' number with them three as well. The final four games in Baltimore looked less and less significant all the time.

In the final games of the season against New York, Henderson was finally turning into himself, hotdogging outrageously with slap catches in the outfield and a weird little skipping run when he scored the homer on Key. Paul Molitor had been impressed that Henderson hadn't done it when he first joined the Jays, showing that Henderson had respect for the organization and where he was going. But if it helped him play better, as far as Molitor was concerned, Henderson could do anything he wanted.

The next afternoon the Jays tightened their grasp on the East, with a 3–1 win against the Yankees, who effectively slipped into third place behind Baltimore. Al Leiter, in his first start since June, retired after pitching six innings of shutout baseball. The next night, however, the Blue Jays lost, relinquishing their last opportunity to clinch at home.

"THE CONSUMMATE BALL PLAYER"

The next chance to clinch would come the following night, September 27. The Jays were going to Milwaukee, and there was a strong chance that they would win the division there. Molitor felt the conflict. "There's an irony involved, but I won't get any special satisfaction out of it. I don't think there's a bad place to win a division title. I've been waiting a long time to do it, so they're all good. Winning in Milwaukee will be a little awkward, though."

It was a very cold night in County Stadium when the Jays faced the Brewers, far too cold for baseball. The crowd was sparse and the pitchers blew constantly on their hands, while players huddled in the dugout.

It was bound to be a significant day for Paul Molitor. He hadn't fared especially well in earlier return visits to Milwaukee, but much was riding on this game. There was pressure on Molitor as there was on no other man in the stadium. He had worked so many years in County Stadium, playing toward a post-season that had eluded him for a decade. County Stadium was the theatre in which he had spent his career — it was where he had entered the majors, where he had ended the 39-game streak, where he had played in over 1,000 games, every home game he'd played between the ages of 21 and 36. It wasn't so much that he was playing for the visiting team now — he had done that before — but rather, that he was playing for the visiting team when the victory could only have meaning for the visiting team. Any result would be bittersweet.

In his first at bat, leading off in the second inning, Molitor swung at the first pitch thrown. He drove it over the left-field fence for the first run of the game. One can talk of special skills and "money players" and of a man rising to a heightened occasion, but the hit seemed predestined. In a town where Molitor had once had a reputation for swinging at first pitches, he had swung at Cal Eldred's first pitch with devastating effect. There was something of a tribute in the hit: to the Brewers, to the stadium, to the city.

In the third inning, the cold skies opened and it began to rain very heavily. Crews came out to put sand around the pitcher's mound and around home plate. It was a significant game and the umpires decided to keep playing it. The few fans, many of them Jays fans who had traveled through the previous night in hopes of seeing the team lock up first place, moved back under the protruding stands, huddling under blankets for warmth. Rob Butler, the Jays' sole native Canadian, stood alone outside the dugout, watching the game in the downpour. Five innings and it could be called a complete game.

By the end of the fifth inning, however, the heavy rain had finally let up, and the game continued. It was as if it had gone into extra innings with the result already decided: a long and strange anticlimax. The tension of the game was less in whether the Jays would win but whether Molitor's homer would stand in all its symbolic glory as the winning run. Although the game ended 2–0 for Toronto, there was something inviolable about that home run. The Jays might add to it, but they couldn't diminish it by allowing a run. Pat Hentgen maintained the shutout. Molitor had decided the game on the first ball pitched to him.

Interviewed after the game about clinching, both Ed Sprague and Jack Morris talked about how significant it was for Molitor. Sprague called him the "consummate ball player." Morris, his own playing days with the Jays likely over, knew what the post-season meant to Molitor. Molitor was, as usual, fairly subdued about the victory. "It was certainly ironic," he allowed. When the Brewers had clinched in '82, they had done so in Baltimore. He had wanted to win the AL East in County Stadium for 15 years, and when he finally did, it was for another team.

One writer called it a "storybook" game, and it was. But there was something more loose in the night, something hinted at in the deluge, the tedium, and the fable-like simplicity of a game that looked as though it had all been played for the sake of a particular pitch and a particular hit.

BAD TIMING

The morning after the Jays clinched the AL East, a bellhop arrived at the door of Molitor's hotel room with newspapers. "How does it look?" Molitor asked. The front page of the *Milwaukee Journal*'s sports section was headlined: "The Book on Molitor: Agent Details Cocaine Use, Tough Talks."

Like a jilted lover, the Milwaukee newspaper seemed to be taking its revenge for his defection, choosing this moment to publish excerpts from the book *The Game behind the Game: Negotiating in the Big Leagues*, by Molitor's longtime agent and financial advisor, Ron Simon. In his chapter on Molitor, Simon discussed Molitor's drug use during 1980 and '81, and said Bud Selig simply hadn't been interested in signing Molitor at the end of the 1992 season. According to Simon, Bud Selig had called Molitor and Robin Yount "wimps" during the 1990 negotiations.

Molitor, in a display of remarkable control, wasn't angry at Simon. He knew the book to be slightly dramatic, but he was still concerned about Simon's own position. Suffering from Parkinson's disease, Simon had decided to write about his involvement in sports contracts while he still could. Molitor had seen the chapter before and knew that it had been available to the Milwaukee press weeks before. He knew, too, that the chapter's contents had been rearranged to highlight Simon's slightly sensationalized account of his drug use. Those were the parts that hurt. He really couldn't understand why the Milwaukee press would pick this moment to dredge up his past.

The drug problem had been chronicled before and Molitor had gone to great lengths to atone for it, again and again contributing his time to speaking to young people about the perils of drug use. As recently as March 1993, Richard Hoffer, writing for the vast audience of *Sports Illustrated*, had called him "still maddeningly confessional about it."

Perhaps the saddest thing about Simon's book and its sudden rise to notoriety is the impression left by the title, that the game of negotiating that goes on behind the scenes is in some sense the real game, what matters most, rather than simply the inevitable consequence of professional sports' popularity and the sums of money that that popularity brings to bear on relationships. Simon's "game" is certainly "real" — Molitor didn't deny any of it — but there are any number of games involved in the game of baseball, and Molitor's long commitment to the Brewers and his community work did much to counteract impressions of self-serving greed.

In a way, it was as if the Milwaukee papers were finally fully aware of what Molitor had meant to the Brewers and, amid the shambles of a team that he'd left, were taking their revenge, on the Brewers as much as on Molitor. At the end of the season, the Brewers would finish 26 games back of the Jays, with 69 wins and a winning percentage of just .426. The fall after Molitor's departure was even more precipitous than the one that had happened almost nine years before when he had missed almost the entire 1984 season with elbow surgery. The youthful team that had shown so much promise in 1992 was little better without Molitor than the team of 1984, or the team of 1987, had been.

BACK TO BALTIMORE

The final, four-game series of the regular season in Baltimore had been anticipated since the All-Star Game. Now, however, after the Jays had won the division in Milwaukee, the games against the Orioles were anticlimactic, as anticlimactic as the games in Milwaukee after September 27.

There was little animosity evident on the part of the Orioles' fans. The only thing unusual about the first game was a tendency for foul balls to end up in the Jays' dugout, a fluke that began with a Jays hitter but was wildly applauded by the crowd. By the end of the night it had happened three times, and Molitor, laughing, equipped himself with a fielder's mitt. It might come in handy — Molitor, daily taking practice at third base, fielding grounders, was awaiting the possibility that he might be playing there in the World Series when the DH position disappeared in the National League park. It was a time to savor the division title and prepare for the championship games ahead. The series against Baltimore lacked drama, and many of the Jays regulars were being rested, giving newcomers a chance to play. In the second inning of the final game, though, the Jays returned in force. Joe Carter led off the inning with a home run and finished it the same way, becoming the first Jay to ever hit two home runs in a single inning. Molitor managed to steal home, once again, in the same inning. When the inning was over, the Jays had piled up eight runs. The offence was definitely ready.

As the Jays faced the post-season, it would seem like half the team had declared they were trying to win it for Molitor. Much like it had with the Brewers during the streak in 1987, Molitor's desire was galvanizing the team to push their game that much further. Joe Carter had said at the start of the season that you had to want to win to have any hope of winning the World Series a second time. Molitor wanted to win a first time. Pat Hentgen and Duane Ward, Jack Morris and Ed Sprague, even Cito Gaston were talking about winning because of how much it meant to Molitor. In the often cynical world of professional sports, it was a very rare thing. It was as if Molitor found a way to place a new value on what the others already had.

SOME REGULAR SEASON NUMBERS

Molitor led the Jays in runs with 121 and led the American League with 211 hits. His 111 RBIS were only 10 behind Carter's 121. His batting average was .332, second only to Olerud's .363 in the American League. With Robbie Alomar at .326, the '93 Blue Jays possessed the three highest batting averages in the American League. The last time that a team had accomplished that was in 1893 in the National League and 1891 in the old

American Association. The Blue Jays' offense really did belong in baseball history, and it reminded Molitor of the 1982 season, when he and Yount and Cooper had each managed over 200 hits. Tony Fernandez had, since 1987, held the Blue Jays record for batting average with .322, but now three teammates had suddenly surpassed it in a single season. Fernandez's own record for 1993 was a creditable .306.

The team's hitting was balanced by its performance on the base paths, where they had also led the American League with 170 stolen bases. Molitor had 22, but was well behind Alomar with 55 and White with 34. Rickey Henderson had 53, but many had come early in the season with Oakland.

Molitor, the first player ever to reach 100 RBIS for the first time at age 37, was also the oldest player ever to record both 20 stolen bases and 20 home runs in the same season. The second oldest player to do it, at 34, was Rickey Henderson, playing on the same team in the same season. Molitor was also the oldest player to ever lead the major leagues in hits. So beautifully balanced was his performance that he joined the very short list of players who had managed 20 homers, 20 stolen bases, and 200 hits in a single season, and was the first from the American League. He had already come to the Jays as just the second man to bat over .300 and steal 300 bases in his career, a feat previously accomplished by Willie Mays.

But Molitor's numbers had been impressive before. The figure that was new was the 22 home runs he had hit during the season, making him the oldest player ever to hit 20 home runs for the first time in his career. He told the *Toronto Star*'s Rosie DiManno, "That was the big surprise, after all these years." In his best seasons, Molitor had managed to hit homers. In '82, when Milwaukee went to the World Series, he had had 19 in the regular season, for his previous career high. That was the year he had hit three homers in a single game against Kansas City. In '87, his most brilliant season, he'd managed 16 in 118 games. But in '91 and '92, when he'd managed to play throughout the year, he'd hit 17 and 12, respectively. Moving down in the batting order will give a consistent hitter more RBIS, and a major market will give recognition, but it's hard to imagine where a player will find more power at 37.

There may have been several contributing factors. Cito Gaston, who wasn't surprised by Molitor's end-of-season stats, had predicted as early as spring training that Molitor's slugging would improve just because he was playing 81 games in SkyDome rather than in County Stadium. The left- and right-field fences in Milwaukee's County Stadium are 362 feet from home plate. The left-center and right-center fences are 392 feet, and the fence at center field is 402 feet. The left-and right-field fences in Toronto's SkyDome are 328 feet from home plate. Left-center and right-center are 375 feet, and center field, 400. A hitter with exceptional control can exploit the 34-foot difference at the extreme left- and right-field fences, and Paul Molitor was nothing if not a hitter with exceptional control. Kansas City's Royals Stadium, where Molitor had homered three times in a single game, had left-and right-field fences only 330 feet from home plate. If Molitor hadn't spent his career in County Stadium, his career stats for homers might have looked very different.

There might be more working in Molitor's favor in 1993 as well. Nineteen ninety-three was a year for hitters. ERAS were up and so were extra-base hits, signalling a trend which some would attribute to a decline in pitching brought about by expansion. There was talk of bringing in pitchers from Cuba. Baseball, not the New World Order, might alter American foreign policy. Others thought it was the ball: the ball was going further in 1993 and it might just be the stitching. It was a year when the baseball itself could turn a skilled hitter into a power hitter, and there was simply no hitter in baseball more skillful than Molitor. In 1991, when he had led the league in hits and runs, he had managed 13 triples. In 1993, leading the league in hits and second in runs, Molitor had hit for only 5 triples. What seemed to be happening was that triples were turning into homers in his stats. Whether the ball was suddenly going further, or the usual fence was 34 feet closer, Molitor was benefiting from it, finding a new niche in the record book in the same year that he was playing for a championship team in a major market.

The most important statistic, however, was that he'd managed to play in nearly every game during the regular season. With that added to the last two seasons with Milwaukee, he was finally putting to rest the idea that he was injury prone. He had, though, played the vast majority of those games at the designated hitter spot, without some of the risks that accompany the regular grind of fielding and throwing. His appearances in the infield had been limited to 23. Staying healthy throughout the season, Molitor had approached his career bests for runs, hits, and batting average.

The final burst in September pushed the 1993 Jays to 95 wins, just one short of the 96 they had posted in 1992, making them seem more competitive with the Braves, Giants, White Sox, and Phillies. But throughout much of the season they had not played like a championship team. In the final home stand against New York, the Jays had seemed like a vastly superior team in every aspect of their game, but for much of the season the two teams had been almost even. When the pitching was good the bats were cold, and when the bats were hot the pitching was weak. Sometimes they were both weak. They had hardly ever come together, but they showed signs in September, signs that the team could repeat its post-season performance.

The question remained: could the offense-rich and pitching-starved Jays continue to compete in the finals, where pitching and defense had traditionally dominated? The pitching had again begun to show weaknesses. In the final four games against Baltimore, both Stottlemyre and Hentgen had struggled in their starts. It was reminiscent of the Brewers in '82. A team could go only so far on batting, and facing the White Sox in the American League Championship Series, the Jays would be facing some very good pitching indeed.

I4

The 1993 ALCS

As the series against Chicago started, Molitor was finally playing in the post-season again, finally getting to play in the games he had left the Brewers to play. After a decade of watching the post-season on television, he was going to be back in the middle of it. There would be pressure, certainly, but it was the pressure that drove his career, a pressure that he could somehow turn into fun.

He had had excellent games against Chicago during the regular season. On April 24, when he was still getting accustomed to SkyDome, he had hit a two-run homer off Rod Bolton. On July 19 in Chicago, he had managed to get four hits, but those hits had mainly come against Bolton as well. Bolton wouldn't be starting against the Jays in this series. Instead, the Jays would be facing Jack McDowell, the American League's leading pitcher, and some very talented younger pitchers, 24-year-old Alex Fernandez and 23-year-old Wilson Alvarez.

The most important issues of the championship would be the pitching and the health of Chicago's Frank Thomas, who had been out of the lineup with a tricep injury. With 41 home runs and a .317 average during the regular season, the first baseman was the key to his team's offense in a way that no single Blue Jay was. Molitor had endeared himself even to

Chicago fans, saying he hoped Frank Thomas would recover and be able to play. He liked to play another team when they were at their best. Molitor was showing more concern for Thomas's well being, and Chicago's hopes, than some of the White Sox players would, but there was a challenge there as well. Molitor never said he didn't want to win — he just wanted to win with Frank Thomas in the Chicago line-up.

Facing Jack McDowell in the first game, Molitor simply took up where he had left off a decade before. By the end of the game, he had four hits, including a two-RBI homer in the seventh inning. In the second game, he had two more hits, establishing an ALCS record of six consecutive hits. Toronto had taken a two-game lead in the series.

DESIGNATED HITTERS

The Chicago series testified to how far the Jays had come and how wise their personnel decisions could be, particularly concerning designated hitters, an area in which Chicago's choices stood as a lesson in contrast. Thomas, unable to play first base in the first two games, went into the lineup as designated hitter in those games, replacing Bo Jackson or George Bell, the usual Chicago DHS. Thomas's replacement at first, Dan Pasqua, was hardly adequate to the task. His bat was flaccid and he committed errors at first.

It was the signal for Jackson and Bell to find a new route into the game. Someone talking about the team spirit of the old Milwaukee Brewers had once contrasted "Harvey's Wallbangers" with Reggie Jackson: "The last time Reggie said 'we' he meant it in the royal sense." The same could be said of Bo Jackson or George Bell, the principal difference being that no one was going to mistake either of them for "Mr. October" at this stage in their careers.

With the White Sox losing the first two games at home and

fans booing the team as they left the field, each DH was quick to take his views about the managing to the press. Jackson claimed some team members had discussed it and decided they were "playing a man short," presumably meaning himself. It was an interesting complaint, but one that no amount of juggling could resolve. Did Jackson think he could play first base? Did he think the injured Thomas should play first base? Did he think he was a better candidate for DH than Frank Thomas?

George Bell wasn't being played at DH either and was talking to reporters, doing everything he could to undermine manager Gene Lamont. With Toronto fans poised for Bell to renew hostilities with his former team, Bell second-guessed them and yet still remained true to himself. He attacked his present team. Bell had lost all respect for Lamont "as a manager and as a man," and, according to Bell, "48 percent of the players" felt the same way.

Lamont, of course, was put in a difficult position by each man's comments. To Lamont, Bell had "bit the hand of one of his biggest backers, maybe his most important backer." Now Lamont would be damned if he played his DHs, and damned if he didn't. If he didn't play them and lost, he might appear to be hurting the team's chances out of spite. If he played them and won, he'd make them look like they'd been right. If he played them and lost, he'd look like he'd been intimidated. With Thomas back at first for game three, Lamont would use Bo Jackson and Warren Newson. At least one Chicago writer thought Bell might have inadvertently helped the team, getting them to play as a unit to win game three.

The discontent of Jackson and Bell revealed much of the frustration of the DH. The DH spends the larger part of the game on the bench, watching others do what he used to do. His only justification is his skill with his bat. He can only affect offense. For Jackson and Bell, fast-fading stars of the game, the frustration of not hitting, and perhaps of watching their team lose as well, was simply too much. They were becoming managers without portfolio to enter somehow into the play of the game, polling fellow players, making pronouncements, second-guessing their manager.

The revolt of the Chicago DHS would highlight just how careful the Jays had been in this area. Of course it's a frustrating position, and the better the player has been, the greater the frustration will be. The signing of Winfield and Molitor showed just how much concern the Jays' management had for character and what they were willing to invest in the position. The two free-agent veterans had proven essential to team spirit. When Chicago came back to even the series by winning the first two games in Toronto, there was some concern. When Cito Gaston had to pull Pat Hentgen after three innings in game three, there was criticism for starting him at home during the series, given his remarkable road record, 12 wins against 3 losses, during the regular season. Similarly, when in game four Gaston left Todd Stottlemyre in for one too many innings — the sixth, in which Chicago scored three runs and took the lead — Gaston was roundly criticized in the press. But he wasn't criticized by a member of the team and the team wasn't booed by the fans. The '93 Jays, like their predecessors of 1992, were consistently reliable in such matters.

Molitor took time to express his respect for the pitching of Wilson Alvarez and Alex Fernandez. He was impressed when Alvarez held the Jays to a single run in a complete-game performance to get Chicago back into the series in the third game. Alvarez had a talent for finding the corner of the plate. Fernandez had a good fastball, which reminded Molitor of the great Jim Palmer, of Orioles' fame. It was Palmer who the Brewers had managed to beat in the last game of the '82 season to win the AL East. Clearly, Molitor's last trip to the post-season, 11 years before, was much on his mind as the Jays, who had pulled ahead again with a 5–3 win in game five, prepared for the sixth game against Chicago. Fernandez would be the starter.

But the Jays' offense was holding. It was too much for McDowell in games one and five, and it would prove to be too much for Fernandez. Game six shaped up as the same kind of taut pitching duel that had taken place in game two between Fernandez and Dave Stewart, during which Fernandez gave one of the best pitching performances of the series in a game the White Sox eventually lost 3–1.

The Chicago fielders committed a series of errors in game six, and the Jays were quick to capitalize. Molitor got on base in the second by being hit by a pitch and eventually got home. He got on base again in the fourth on an error and then made it home on another one. In the ninth, with Fernandez retired, Carter singled, Olerud reached base on yet another error, and Molitor drove them home with a triple. The final score was 6–3.

The Jays had won their second ALCS in two years, triumphing in what might be considered the last pure league championship, before realignment would create three divisions in each league and wild-card spots would multiply and cheapen the playoffs. In the players' comments after the win, Molitor's popularity was evident. Dave Stewart, the MVP for the ALCS, called him "my favorite player." He was happiest for Molitor that they had won the series. After 11 years, Molitor was going back to the show.

They would have four days' rest before the World Series was to start at SkyDome and while the NLCS was decided. The next night, October 14, the Atlanta Braves and Philadephia Phillies met in Philadelphia. Either team would pose problems for the Jays. With Atlanta, the Jays' hitters would be facing the best starting rotation in baseball, while with Philadelphia, the Jays' pitchers would be facing tremendously disciplined hitting.

The outcome of the game answered players' and fans' questions alike. The Phillies had come back from the humiliation of game two, in which they were beaten 14 to 5, had come back from a 2 to 1 deficit, to clinch at home in the sixth game.

15

Styles and Substance:
The 1993 World Series

There are probably no two teams in baseball more superficially unalike than the Jays and the Phillies. There are differences that strike you immediately, even before they've begun to play ball. The Jays embody their city's devotion to multiculturalism, money, and manners. The Jays are the most culturally and ethnically diverse team in baseball, with black and white Americans supplemented by Dominicans and Puerto Ricans, a Jamaican and a Canadian. Cito Gaston is the only black manager to ever win a World Series. If pitching is a position that remains dominated by white players, then the Blue Jays are exceptional in this regard as well. The mix on the Phillies is more suggestive of the early days of Jackie Robinson. The Phillies were the last major league ball team to hire a black player, and even since then the practice has hardly caught on.

The Blue Jays are, almost to a man, well groomed. It is very much part of a corporate style, and in fact they've been called "team briefcase." When a reporter once asked Jack Morris to sum up the Jays in one word, he replied, "business-like." The reporter wasn't sure the attitude was appropriate, so he shopped it around the team. When Molitor was asked what he thought of it, he thought it was fine. At a White House reception hosted by George Bush after the '92 win, only rancher Morris appeared in blue jeans and a cowboy hat. If the Phillies were to enjoy the honor in '93, Bill Clinton might think he was at a rural cookout in Arkansas. What keeps the Phillies from looking like a '50s team, however, is the hair.

Many of the Phillies are unshaven, with long rumpled locks drifting out from their caps. The attitude to grooming might extend to fitness. John Kruk, the West Virginian first baseman, dominates the team's visual image, by sheer size and squalor. Kruk is undoubtedly in *some* kind of good physical shape, otherwise he wouldn't be doing what he does, but he brings back to baseball something of the sheer sense of appetite and excess that hung about Babe Ruth. In the last game against Atlanta, Kruk had torn the thigh of his uniform. He wore the pants as a kind of badge until the end of the game. Outfielder Lenny Dykstra has carried the old baseball habit of chewing tobacco to new lengths. Watching Dykstra in a close-up, a viewer might believe Dykstra has enough chaw in his mouth to sustain a whole nineteenth-century team. And that is ultimately what the Phillies suggest: a nineteenth-century baseball team, a rustic one at that, come back to repossess the game in the name of fun.

Their manager, Jim Fregosi, is an old-fashioned manager who used to be an old-fashioned ball player. Back in 1967, Dick Williams, manager of the Boston Red Sox, had benched first baseman George Scott until he lost weight. Fregosi, then shortstop for the California Angels, protested to the press: "We have nine managers in this league and one dietician." When Williams managed Boston to an American League pennant win that year, he sent Fregosi a note that read, "I guess the dietician won."

In the intervening decades, though, Fregosi's attitude didn't seem to have changed. There were tense moments during the

'93 World Series when he would duck down in the dugout for a few puffs of a cigarette. It was part of the Phillies' charm. Winning wasn't worth changing. They would win or lose on their own terms.

Their closer, Mitch "Wild Thing" Williams, seemed to think striking out three batters in a row, in the manner of a Duane Ward or a Tom Henke, was an act of cowardice, the "playing safe" of corporate baseball. In Williams's view, risk was the soul of the game. He would load the bases almost as a matter of course, expecting double plays and fly balls to conclude things. Although somehow Williams's method seemed to work, starter Curt Schilling, the Phillies' best pitcher, would cover his head with a towel when Williams was on the mound, as though unable to watch. During the series, you could never be sure if it was another one of the Phillies' jokes.

The Blue Jays had recruited the cream of the free-agent crop. The Phillies had hired free agents for whom there was little demand. The Jays' payroll, at around $50 million, was double that of the Phillies, which hovered around $26 million. The Jays looked like an All-Star team and the Phillies looked like they belonged in an industrial league.

Molitor captured the absurdity of the image war perfectly, declaring, "I'll bet we have more cellular phones than they do." Laughing, he found a way to gently ridicule the images of both teams, describing himself and his teammates as "genteel." Molitor was prepared to enjoy it all, just as the Phillies seemed to be doing. "Maybe this is all by design," he reflected. "It seems like they do work at their image a lot. If it causes a distraction up until game time, if it causes people to talk about things other than pure baseball, then it's a good thing."

The Phillies reminded Molitor of the 1982 Brewers, the last team he had gone to the World Series with. They were both teams around which the word "zoo" kept appearing. Apart from the Phillies' character and characters, however, there was something of the same muscle-bound, baseball-bashing quality the old Brewers had had. Teams don't get into the World Series by passing a dress code. The Phillies had combined for more runs than any other team in baseball.

What the Jays and the Phillies had in common was determination and tremendous offensive capability. Neither had been expected to be in the 1993 World Series. Neither had even been expected to win its division, and once they'd done that, neither had been favored to win a league championship.

The Blue Jays had initially dropped or lost so much of their personnel that 1993 was thought by many to be a rebuilding year. They'd suffered spotty pitching and sometimes spotty hitting, but somehow they'd always found it within themselves to come back. But the Blue Jays had a record of regular season success. They had advanced to the ALCS in four of the past five seasons, and 1993 was the third time in a row.

The Phillies had gone from nowhere to the World Series in a year. The 1992 Phillies had finished last in the NL East, with a mere 70 wins, 26 games behind the Pirates. Since 1988, the Phillies had finished last in their division three times, in a tie for fourth once, and third once. In defeating the Atlanta Braves in the 1993 NLCS, they'd defeated the team that many thought would win the World Series, to which the Braves had advanced in the two previous seasons. Either the Phillies had done the Jays a tremendous favor, or they were so blessed that they couldn't lose.

In the first two games of the series, the images would start to haunt the Jays and their fans. There were players among the Phillies who were every bit as good in the clutch as there were among the Jays. What was most troubling was their consistency at the plate. The Phillies and the Jays had comparable success in generating runs, but they did it in very different ways. The superficial differences in style concealed the real difference in approaches to the game.

The Jays believed intently in the stolen base and the sacrifice. It had generated remarkable run counts for them. Their life was on the base paths, and their philosophy was to get on them and keep moving. Henderson, in the midst of a bad season, was simply the greatest base stealer of all time; Alomar, with youth on his side, had the most stolen bases on the team; White had tremendous speed, and in the ALCS against Chicago he had produced a .444 batting average, the best on the team; Molitor was an artist, as good on the bases as he was at the plate. The Jays had combined to steal 170 bases during the regular season, the Phillies just 91. The Jays believed, too, in the sacrifice, and Joe Carter was its master. He had the most valuable .254 batting average in the majors. The Phillies hardly ever sacrificed. Instead, they waited.

If someone were to pick a most valuable person for the Phillies, Lenny Dykstra aside, it would probably be their hitting instructor, Denis Menke, the man who seventeen years before had managed Paul Molitor for the Burlington Bees in the Midwest League. The Phillies had a way of wearing down a pitcher. The method was simple: never swing at a bad pitch and tip everything foul that you can. It's of course far harder to do in reality than it is on paper, but the key Phillies — Dykstra, Kruk, Dave Hollins, Darren Daulton, Pete Incaviglia, and Jim Eisenreich — had absolutely mastered it. If the Jays wore down a pitcher from the base paths, the Phillies did it from the batter's box.

This technique didn't take extraordinary athletic prowess. It took discipline, a discipline at the plate that the Phillies' notorious image as wildmen served to conceal. They had used the technique in defeating the Atlanta Braves, the team with the best starting rotation in baseball. For a team that was weak in middle relief, and the Jays had suffered there all year, it could be disastrous.

The Phillies had piled up remarkable base-on-ball counts

throughout the regular season by not swinging at bad pitches. The Phillies had walked 665 times, the Jays, 588. What it meant was that a good pitcher might have to throw over 30 pitches to get out of an inning. Not only were the pitchers frustrated and exhausted, but they also found that the only way to get strikes was to hand the Phillies pitches they might have a chance of hitting. Given those chances, the Phillies would take them to the limit.

Juan Guzman exited after just five innings in game one, having thrown 116 pitches. His record-setting tendency to wild pitches played well to the Phillies, though reliever Al Leiter and the hitters managed to get a Toronto win. Dave Stewart, usually stingy, handed the Phillies five runs in the third inning of game two. He had started by walking the first two batters. When Eisenreich homered with two men on, the Phillies had built a lead that would prove insurmountable. Stewart lasted six innings and threw 122 pitches.

What this might foretell for the Jays' fortunes could be read in the ALCS. Guzman had won his starts in games one and five; Stewart, MVP for the series, had won his in two and six. They were the best the Jays had, and, in the ALCS, they had seemed like they might be all the Jays had.

THE DH AND THE
NATIONAL LEAGUE PARK

The Jays were going to Philadelphia with the series tied at one. Now they were facing the special difficulty of the National League park, where they wouldn't have the use of the designated hitter. It always comes as a sudden shock to American League teams to have pitchers hitting and DHs sitting. Ever since the American League adopted the position in 1973, it had meant controversy. The current policy of the majors is to follow the rules of the home team, which means that games played in AL parks use AL rules, while games in NL parks use theirs. While NL managers would complain about having to adapt, digging up an extra hitter for the AL games, it changed the lineup for AL teams.

The policy is particularly galling to the Blue Jays and their fans. For two seasons, the seasons that saw the team go to the World Series, the designated hitters had been the most popular players on the Jays. Technically, there is no ambiguity about the DH — he is a machine for hitting baseballs. But in landing Winfield and Molitor, the Jays had somehow found the spirit of baseball, had given the richest traditions of the game to the city. The significance of the position for them is apparent in what they are willing to pay for designated hitters. Paul Molitor was being paid $4.5 million per season to play a position that didn't exist in the National League (this might be factored in when contemplating the salary difference between the Jays and the Phillies: Molitor's salary alone accounted for almost one-fifth of the difference). In Philadelphia, Molitor could be watching from the bench and making occasional appearances as a pinch hitter, or taking up duties in the infield, replacing a regular defender and again risking the injuries that had threatened his career before.

For Cito Gaston, the choices were difficult ones. Molitor could replace Olerud at first base, a position Molitor had played during 23 regular-season games. Molitor was better against left-handed pitching than Olerud, but it would mean benching the AL's leading batter. To start Molitor at third base, replacing Ed Sprague, the move most people had expected since the Jays clinched the division, was to put him at a position he hadn't played since before the shoulder surgery of 1990. He would be a defensive liability, and, perhaps worse, he'd be risking injury. There was a chance that Molitor would play at third, mused Gaston, "but I'd certainly like to stay with defense and Paul has not played over there all year." Gaston had considered using Molitor at third during games against Baltimore: "I changed my mind because that's all we would need is for Paul to get hurt. I'm sure Paul wouldn't mind either way because he just wants to win. I'm pretty sure Sprague's the same way. I think it will be dictated by the way the games go." Gaston's conservatism about fielding seemed to be making the choice one of Molitor or Olerud. The apparent indecision over the DH was shaping up to be divisive. As the ALCS had shown, the position can be a breeding ground for frustration, and that frustration is never greater than in the World Series. For the DH, the American League playoffs may represent the most important contribution he can make to his team.

Gaston was undoubtedly the most successful manager ever to have his every move questioned. After taking over as manager of the Jays in 1989, he had won the AL East in four out of five years, and now, for the second time, he had won the ALCS to go on to the World Series. But he was constantly being second guessed, even pre-guessed, in the media. Those who had wanted Stottlemyre dropped from the rotation were now crying for Henderson's demotion to the bench so that Molitor could take his place in left field. Gaston adamantly resisted: "Unless everyone is dead on this team, Molitor will not play left field." Gaston had a much clearer picture of Molitor's elbow and shoulder than fans and the media did, and there was no way he'd have Molitor throwing from the outfield. But for Molitor, it was getting demeaning.

Much of Gaston's success has come from an unwillingness to make changes, from a tendency instead to stick with his players and with his lineup. At times it means a pitcher will stay in a game just a little too long, or a batter will strike out when another might have pinch-hit for him. Generally, though, Gaston's decisions are right, a fact underscored by his record. With an extraordinary winning percentage, Gaston should be a regular contender for manager of the year. He isn't, and whether the reasons are racial or a tendency to devalue the skills needed to coach a team with the talent of the Blue Jays doesn't matter. He is, however, just too good to deserve the malicious second-guessing that he always gets.

There was a strong bond between Molitor and Gaston. The manager reminded Molitor of his favorite coach from his years with the Brewers, the man with whom he'd enjoyed the success of the 1982 season. "I kind of put him in a class with Harvey Kuenn," explained Molitor. "Cito's a guy who relaxes and understands his team, a guy who looks to his players almost like sons, protects them, knows who to give rope to and who to draw the line with, a guy who commands a lot of respect." For Molitor, Gaston was the key to the team's success: "This is a team with a wonderful atmosphere and it's because of the manager. Cito Gaston has the knack of keeping everyone happy and, in return, everybody is willing, even anxious, to go to the wall for him."

So one doesn't disagree lightly with the decisions of Cito Gaston. It's even more difficult for a person like Molitor. He has never hesitated to put team interests ahead of his personal goals, a trait constantly in evidence since he decided 17 seasons ago to stay in single A rather than take a guaranteed spot in triple A because his team had a chance for a championship.

At first, he was philosophical and understanding about the DH decision. He knew that Gaston was concerned that a new position in the infield might distract Molitor from his hitting. "If a player is uncomfortable defensively," Molitor observed, "it takes up all his attention and it could affect his offence. It could happen. In all the new positions I've learned in the various spring trainings, it takes so much of your focus that I would get off to a poor start offensively." He was doing everything he could to support his manager, but he *knew* that

Working out at first base during the World Series.

P. POWER, THE TORONTO STAR

the right decision was to have both him and Olerud play. The struggle was not with Olerud, or with his friend Ed Sprague, the only reasonable choice for the bench, but with Cito Gaston, however great the respect between the two men.

As Toronto drove deeper into the World Series, however, Molitor became increasingly outspoken, at least by his standards, an ever more important presence in the Blue Jays' chemistry. He wanted to play third and he was making his views about the benching known, as subtly as he could. It's typical of his consummate diplomacy that he argued his case without embarrassing Gaston, managing to treat it as a misunderstanding. "I think his concerns are a little overdramatized," Molitor commented. "My skills aren't what they once were, but I think the risk of injury is minimal. Sure it could happen more if you're on the field, but I don't think it's that much of a risk."

The microscope of the World Series is such that it's easier to talk to the media than to the other people involved. Without crossing the line of insubordination, Molitor was saying everything he could to get into the lineup, while keeping John Olerud there as well.

One senses that Molitor was fighting to overcome all the frustrations of his career in his careful comments to the press. The moment that he played for, the moment that he had joined the Jays for, seemed to be slipping from his grasp. Three weeks earlier, when he had clinched the AL East in Milwaukee, he had awoken to face renewed accounts of his ancient difficulties with cocaine. Now, in the midst of the World Series, he was being reminded of his fragility, the proneness to injury that had seen him miss over 500 games while with the Brewers. Coming off one of the best seasons of his career and an ALCS in which he had set a record for consecutive hits, Molitor was being treated like a broken baseball player.

In game three, Gaston decided to put Molitor in at first, benching Olerud. It was apparent that Molitor felt the injustice of Olerud being benched. Now possessing the highest batting average in baseball, Olerud had previously faced benching during the 1992 series to get Dave Winfield into the lineup in the National League park. Before the game, Molitor played catch with the neglected Olerud. "It's probably to Cito's advantage that he's dealing with unselfish people," Molitor remarked. "John is way past me in terms of humbleness. For me, I've *learned* it. When I came up, I was more stats-oriented. I wanted to do things, sometimes, for the wrong reasons. But I watched and learned what's important. With John, it seems to come kind of natural."

Molitor went into the third game with extraordinary focus. In the first inning he hit Danny Jackson for a triple, scoring Henderson and White. With one of his patented sacrifice flies, Carter pulled Molitor home for the third Jay run, before Molitor had ever had to play first base. In the third inning, Molitor hit a solo home run into the Jays' bullpen for a 4–0 lead. By the end of the game, he had added another hit, another RBI and another run in a Toronto effort that concluded with a score of 10–3, despite the loss from the lineup of the American League batting champion.

Molitor is almost a zen master with a bat, almost in communion with the ball. Gaston has said, "I don't know how to pitch to him. I don't know if a lot of people know how to pitch to him." A few pitchers had seemed particularly hard to hit, including Mike Boddicker and knuckleballer Tom Candiotti, both of whom had unusual pitches. Sometimes Molitor also had trouble with rookies — it was a rookie who had stopped the hitting streak — which suggested that part of it was how much time Molitor spent watching. The most important parts of Molitor's offensive arsenal were his eyes and his mind. His knowledge of pitchers around the league was encyclopedic and acute. Something that contributed to his performance in the '93 World Series was Molitor's opportunity to build on that knowledge during spring training. The Jays and Phillies trained close to one another and played each other frequently. He had also faced Danny Jackson in the past, when Jackson pitched for the Royals.

After the game Molitor said, "I really didn't feel any pressure. I knew it might be my only chance to play." It was what Molitor would always say when the pressure was greatest. It was his way of defusing it. He had gone into a World Series game with the unthinkable burden of somehow providing his usual offensive contribution and making up John Olerud's as well. He had, batting .750 for the game. He was making the most of whatever chances came his way.

He had, in the eyes of many, made Cito Gaston look like a genius for playing him at first, but he had done something more significant. He had made himself indispensable. It would be very difficult for Gaston to bench Molitor in games four and five, games in which Olerud's remarkable stats against right-handed pitchers would be needed. Nonetheless, following game three, Gaston still seemed determined to bench Molitor for the next two, granting only that Olerud was "going to have a tough time following Molitor's act."

When the roster for game four appeared, Olerud was back at first, but Molitor's contribution the night before had its effect — that, and perhaps the last-minute talk he had with Gaston. Gaston had finally made the decision to bench Ed Sprague in favor of Molitor in the National League park, a move that most of the Jays and their fans had assumed when the Jays clinched in Milwaukee. Sprague, with a single in game one and an RBI in game three, had a series average of .083. Molitor's was .545. How many errors could Molitor make at third base? When asked how he'd manage a throw to first, Molitor joked that he might settle for passing the ball to the pitcher.

There is no relationship between what Molitor did and what Bo Jackson and George Bell had done a week before, no question that what he was struggling for was an ultimate victory for his team, whatever his personal interest in the outcome. Molitor phrases things very differently, and, perhaps above all, he's right.

THE FIRING OF LARRY HISLE

Molitor would show the same willingness to influence team decisions when rumors began that batting coach Larry Hisle would be dismissed at the end of the 1993 season. In the middle of the World Series, *Toronto Sun* columnist Bob Elliott revealed that sources in the Jays' organization had leaked that Hisle's stay with the Jays would soon be history. Cito Gaston was strikingly noncommittal on the subject, lending credence to speculation that he was responsible for Hisle's impending dismissal. The idea seemed ridiculous. Hisle, recovering from offseason heart surgery, had been unable to contribute as fully as he might in the early part of the season, leaving some of the batting coaching duties to an already overworked Cito Gaston. But, once recovered, Hisle had worked hard and had managed to coach the hitting of a team that had produced the three best batting averages in baseball on a single team for the first time in a century.

Hisle and Molitor had been friends 16 years before. The veteran Hisle had helped the rookie Molitor with his hitting then, and the Jays' success was testimony to his skill. Hisle was still a help to Molitor, a perfectionist who talked with every coach and hitter he could about the art of hitting. For Molitor, the rumors of dismissal were another case of "bad timing," the same thing that had happened only a few weeks before when the Milwaukee press decided to reexplore his drug history the morning after he had finally managed to clinch in Milwaukee. Molitor used his growing stature to support Hisle, just as he had used it for Olerud on the issue of benching in

Philadelphia. "It's poor judgment, a poor decision, poor timing," complained Molitor. "I don't know who could leak something like that at a time like this. I feel for Larry because we're in the middle of something like this. There's no reason for him not to be back. The hitters have had a lot of success. He's committed to his work."

"To me," Molitor continued, "a hitting coach is a guy who knows his hitters, makes himself available, He's an encourager, he's positive, he knows when a guy is off track and he knows how to get him back on track. Larry possesses all those things. I love the man." In the offseason, the Jays management would decide to retain Hisle and the rest of their coaching staff.

In making his views known, Molitor was becoming an important voice in the Jays' decisions, a legitimate defender of players' and fans' feelings and interests. His tremendous popularity with fans was due as much to his personality as it was to his accomplishments as a player. Molitor presents himself as capable and knowledgeable, with none of the arrogance that one might expect from one of the most productive players in the game. As a longtime players' representative and a veteran of the bargaining in 1990, he is as good a clubhouse lawyer as one is likely to find. It is the same diplomacy that benefited the Jays at critical moments in 1993. It is the same kind of control that he displays in the batting box.

GAMES 4 AND 5: A STUDY IN CONTRASTS

The change that put Molitor at third was a wise decision. As game four unfolded, the Jays were going to need all the offense they could find to stay in the game. Defense wouldn't be an issue.

Game four will go down in the history of the series as one of the ugliest and most entertaining games ever played, a parade of inept pitchers in a late-starting game on a rain-soaked field that went on to become the longest game in World Series history, with a final score that might have been more appropriate in a defensively well-played Super Bowl.

In the first inning, the Jays staked Todd Stottlemyre to a three-run lead off Tommy Greene, just as they had the night before for Pat Hentgen. In the bottom of the first, though, Stottlemyre gave up four runs. Before the game ended in a score of 15–14, 11 pitchers had taken the mound and one commentator was calling it World Series batting practice. The only error of the game occurred at third base, but it happened when the Jays were at bat. The Phillies' Dave Hollins missed a hard grounder that Molitor hit for a double, scoring Joe Carter in a wild eighth inning that saw the Jays score six runs, five against Phillies closer Mitch Williams, to come back from a score of 14–9 to win the game. Phillies pitcher Curt Schilling was still sitting in the dugout with a towel covering his head whenever Williams pitched, but what had so far looked like more of that wacky Phillies humor was starting to look serious.

Baseball purists and pitching careers apart (Stottlemyre, Greene, and Williams had career-damaging turns at best), Molitor may have suffered more than anyone else from the pitching. He was struck on the knee in the sixth inning. Whereas Gaston had worried about injuries in the field, Molitor came closest at the plate. Injuries are never far from Molitor's mind, and later he would describe his fears: "When it hit me, my knee went totally numb. Immediately when something like that happens, you fear the worst. Thankfully, after 20 seconds, it started to get better. I've had some swelling in the kneecap. After being hit, I had a little trouble with my range and my motion, but certainly it's nothing serious. Luckily, there was no fracture." Molitor's luck was holding. He had survived first base, he was surviving third base, and now he had survived a wild pitch.

Todd Stottlemyre and Tommy Greene would each leave the game — and the series — with an ERA of 27. Greene, though, managed to shine in one offensive statistic, the only kind available. The single he hit against Stottlemyre gave him a perfect World Series batting average of 1.000. Al Leiter, too, had a perfect batting average, and his game ERA was only 10.13. The pitching was so bad, even the pitchers were hitting it. In Stottlemyre's sole at bat, Greene walked him.

For Molitor, a lover of offense, there was nothing to complain about. He thought it was the most exciting win he'd ever been a part of. The longest game in World Series history had set a new record for runs, 29, topping by 7 a record that had stood since 1936. The teams had also set a record for the most runs in the first four games, 65, topping a 61-year-old record by 9 runs. Of those runs, the Jays had 37, the Phillies 28. The Jays and Phillies had worked through each other's starting rotations and the Jays had come out 9 runs ahead.

The Jays' offensive machine was working brilliantly. By the end of game four, Molitor was leading the team with a series average of .533, but others weren't far behind. Fernandez's average was .467, Alomar's .444, and White's .413. Carter's was .353, Henderson's was .333, and Olerud's was an even .300. Game five, the last Phillies' home stand, would be the Jays' first chance to clinch their second World Series.

As things turned out, though, that fifth game was the only game of the series to be decided by World Series-class pitching. Curt Schilling and Juan Guzman each gave his team's best pitching performance of the series, but Schilling's was the better. While Guzman allowed two runs in seven innings, Schilling allowed five hits and no runs, battling the Jays' hitters to a complete-game shutout.

Molitor's second night at third had no effect on the outcome. Schilling dominated the Jays from beginning to end, becoming only the second pitcher to shut them out in 1993.

Practising at third base during the World Series.
P. POWER, THE TORONTO STAR

He was keeping the Phillies' hopes alive as if he was the only pitcher who could do it. Perhaps he was. A fan in the upper bleachers held aloft a sign reading "Will Pitch Middle Relief For Food." It was as if Schilling were pitching his own save, keeping the game out of the hands of the Phillies' bullpen. It was one night he wouldn't have to put a towel over his head when Mitch Williams came in to close.

At the end of the game, Molitor felt the loss. He could think back to his last trip to the World Series, when the Brewers twice had had the chance to win and twice the Cardinals had beaten them. This was the third World Series game he'd played where his team had the chance to win it all and hadn't. Looking dejected, but still the best kind of competitor, he spoke to Schilling in passing to congratulate him on his performance. "He said, 'Great job.' To me, that's what baseball's about," Schilling told reporters.

In Toronto there would be two more chances to win, if more than one was needed.

GAME 6

There were 52,195 in attendance at SkyDome for game six on Saturday, October 23. Following the great DH debate and his performances in Philadelphia, Molitor's popularity was soaring. It was now spreading well beyond the fans of Milwaukee and Toronto. Jim Monroe, an assistant district attorney who had traveled from Canton, New York, for the game, carried a placard declaring "Molitor vs the Phillies."

By the end of the first inning, the game was looking almost like a carbon copy of game three in Philadelphia, when Molitor's first-inning triple had scored two runs, and he got home on Carter's sacrifice fly. In game six Molitor again hit a triple in his first at bat, but only White, walked again, was on base to take advantage of it. Another sacrifice fly by Carter scored Molitor. Again the Blue Jays left the first inning with a three-run lead. The Phillies picked up a run in the fourth, but the Jays regained the three-run cushion with another run in the bottom of the inning.

When Molitor came to bat in the fifth inning, there were already chants of "M V P . . . M V P" erupting in the stands. He responded and hit a solo home run, just as he had in game three in Philadelphia. He wanted to show his excitement, but he thought twice, he always thought twice, and decided not to. He looked up to where his family sat to catch the eye of his father. His father wasn't in the stands — the tension had driven him out of his seat. Dick Molitor watched his son on a television monitor in the corridors around the stadium, and it was there that he saw Paul look up at him.

The Jays' lead of 5–1 looked commanding, but the Phillies were too good a team to simply roll over. In the seventh inning the Jays' pitching began to unravel. The Phillies were ready to pounce. Dave Stewart walked Kevin Stocker and then gave up a single to Mickey Morandini, turning over the Phillies rotation. Dykstra took the count to 3–1 and then hit his fourth home run of the series, making the score an uncomfortably close 5–4 for the Jays. Danny Cox came in to relieve Stewart, but there was no relief for the Jays. Cox gave up a walk and three singles to the five batters he faced, allowing the tying run and loading the bases. Relieving Cox, Al Leiter allowed the go-ahead run on Pete Incaviglia's sacrifice fly.

The Jays held the Phillies to the one-run lead until the bottom of the ninth. The top of the Jays rotation was facing Mitch Williams, the erratic closer who'd allowed them that final wild victory in game four. When Williams walked Rickey Henderson for his first trip to the bases in the game, he didn't just put the tying run on base. With no one out, he put the greatest base stealer the game had ever known on base, and if

Henderson had seldom played near his customary level while with Toronto, he was a player who could sometimes perform magic. There are no words to describe the tension in Sky-Dome during that inning. With every batter who got to the plate, Williams would be facing the potential winning run.

Devon White flew out and Henderson was held at first. As he came to bat, Molitor thought about trying to hit a home run, but he controlled the impulse. "You play the percent-ages," he would later say. Molitor hit a line drive to shallow right-centre, hitting it so hard and fast that he could only get to first and Henderson could only get to second.

The pressure or the mathematics, maybe both, was too much for Williams. There was only one out. You could have a debate about who was the best base runner of his generation using just the names of the men he'd put on base. Williams had gotten himself into a position where another flaw in his game would cost the Phillies the season. Lined up before him were Carter, the Jays' RBI and home run leader, Olerud, the American League batting champion, and Alomar and Fernan-dez, whose averages during the Series had hovered in the .400s. One way or another, Williams wouldn't have to face all of them.

John Kruk had been joking about sudden death since the Jays gained their third win in game four. "If you're going to die, it might as well be sudden," he had said. For Williams it was. His first two pitches to Carter were balls. The third was a called strike, a fastball high and to the outside of the plate. Awaiting the next pitch, Carter, like Molitor before him, calmed himself with the thought that all he needed was a base hit. Anticipating, Henderson and Molitor began to stretch their leads at second and first.

The next pitch was a slider, low and inside, and Carter reached down for it, caught it, and drove it deep towards the left-field fence. Henderson and Molitor and Carter were run-

Coming home on Joe Carter's home run.

D. LOEK, THE TORONTO STAR

ning. Carter was rounding first when it left the park, and he was suddenly leaping, taking huge bouncing jumps around the base paths, the same wild bounces he had made a year before at first base in Atlanta. Molitor was leaping when he rounded third, in midair when he slapped the hand of third base coach Nick Leyva.

Afterwards, Molitor reflected, "A lot of us were, in the back of our mind, thinking about a home run. We didn't want to go to a seventh game. I know for myself, you almost fight the notion of trying to hit a home run. Then Joe hits it and . . . it's one of those instantaneous feelings where everything starts to sink in. You run the gamut of emotions. Then you just join the mob scene."

It was the kind of moment that Molitor had always played for, one of baseball's minor, transcendent miracles when things converge to defeat probability. Carter's was only the second home run in baseball history to win a World Series, 33 years after Bill Mazeroski had done it for the Pirates. Molitor was as joyous at Carter's big hit as he could be, as joyous as he could have been if he'd hit it himself. With tears in their eyes, Molitor and Cito Gaston hugged one another.

Molitor was chosen Most Valuable Player for the series. Devon White could joke, "He took it from me, literally." It had been that kind of performance. Winning the award for Most Valuable Player, Molitor declared, "More than anything, I have a feeling of thankfulness."

He was quick to apply the perspectives of real life, though, beyond his own particular field of dreams. He spoke of the sorrow he felt at the deaths of the Cleveland pitchers at the start of the season, and of coach Rich Hacker's near-fatal accident at the time of the All-Star Game, and of his joy at being part of Carter's moment of glory.

His moment of triumph was not simply his, and he was keenly aware of his team, of Gaston and Carter, of men who

World Series MVP.

M. SLAUGHTER, THE TORONTO STAR

furthered his career, of Larry Hisle and Denis Menke and Bud Selig, of his vast family, his parents, his sisters, and Linda and Blaire.

Accepting the award, Molitor showed how keenly he felt his baseball history. His greatest joy seemed to come not from his own achievements but from being there to see Carter's hit. He compared the bottom-of-the-ninth, game-winning homer to Bill Mazeroski's similar feat in the 1960 playoff. Carter told him, "This one's for you."

Bud Selig, now acting commissioner of baseball, who a year before had been able to offer Molitor only a pay cut of one third of his salary, was there to congratulate him in the dressing room. The favor Selig had done him couldn't be clearer.

As Molitor went to exit the clubhouse for the interview room, he noticed that he had a champagne bottle in one hand and a beer can in the other. "I better not take these with me. It might not look too good," he said, already concerned about appearances after the moment of triumph. Maybe it wouldn't have looked good, though there are few contemporary athletes who might consider that at such a moment, but the symbolism of the two drinks was perfect. One wasn't really better than the other, they were just different. They could symbolize the two teams in the series, the two cities where he'd spent his professional career, and, above all, the man himself. Molitor's talent might be the champagne of baseball, but it was the work ethic, the persistence, and the day-in and day-out struggle that had kept his talent developing, kept it fresh, kept it alive, that he might one day come to enjoy this moment.

In the streets of Toronto, a million fans celebrated the victory with few acts of violence or serious accidents. Two thousand miles away, in the small Saskatchewan city of Saskatoon, the victory became the occasion for rioting, and an unruly mob of four thousand ran through the streets, breaking windows and looting. Police made 14 arrests.

16

Other Dimensions

On November 10, the results of the voting for American League MVP were announced. Chicago's Frank Thomas was the winner, but the list of runners-up said more about the real strengths of the Blue Jays, who occupied half of the first six positions. Molitor came in second, John Olerud came in third, and Roberto Alomar came in sixth. In 1992, when Molitor may have been *relatively* more valuable to the Brewers, he had finished tenth. Major markets and post-season play could certainly get a player more attention. Later in the month, the Toronto chapter of the Baseball Writers of America picked Molitor as the Blue Jays' most valuable player. Olerud was in second place, and Alomar, who had won the award in the two previous years, was in third. Even apart from statistics, Molitor had earned it. He was infused with a desire to win that the team as a whole might have otherwise lacked, he was the most consistent player in tough situations, and he was the man whose work ethic had kept the team going when it seemed to lag. The team had afforded him an opportunity that he hadn't had in 11 years. In Toronto there was no sense that he was the "franchise player," as there might have been in Milwaukee, but he had given the franchise another quality.

Paul Molitor had accomplished much in the '93 season. His

new-found durability at the DH position, along with his spectacular statistics, could help lead to a place in the Hall of Fame. He had done much, too, for the American League's case on behalf of the designated hitter. Ron Rapoport, writing in the *Los Angeles Daily News*, put it best:

> A clearer demonstration of what the DH adds to baseball can scarcely be imagined than the one Molitor provided during the Series. Had it not been for the existence of the DH, of course, none of this could have happened. Had it not been for the DH, the Blue Jays would not have been interested in signing Molitor in the first place.
>
> Had it not been for the DH, in fact, there is no telling where Molitor might have been or what he might have done this season.
>
> . . . Instead, Molitor became one of baseball's most heartening success stories this season.

Molitor's performance in the World Series could have some effect on the DH controversy. He was a superannuated infielder who achieved a series batting average of .500, tied records for World Series hits (with Roberto Alomar and Billy Martin) and extra-base hits (with Devon White and Willie Stargell), and became the first designated hitter to win the MVP award. His record spoke volumes, not only about the DH position, but about the growing disparity between the haves and have-nots of baseball. To have the best designated hitter in baseball is something for which the Jays have paid heftily. They were able to sign Molitor not only by offering the promise of success, but by offering twice as much money as the Milwaukee Brewers were able to find for him.

That World Series victory was significant not only for Molitor, but also for the future of the position that he played and the kinds of markets that he had worked in. As the gap widens between teams in major and minor markets, there are fewer major players working in small market franchises. Free agency takes the older ones and arbitration decisions make the younger ones unaffordable. If the Phillies are part of a large but divided market, they had demonstrated perhaps just how far a team could go on heart, determination, and a $25 million payroll. If the '93 series had been the last of its kind, the last series to be played before altered divisions introduce wild cards, it was also among those in which a team's wealth would determine whether or not it was even in the running.

At some point, the problem of the DH and the problem of the small-market teams might come to appear related. Molitor was keenly aware of how the two problems affected baseball. On one hand, the designated hitter has both added to the offensive game and permitted significant careers to continue. The list of hitters includes Molitor's old teammates like Larry Hisle, Cecil Cooper, and Gorman Thomas, and recent DHs like George Brett and Bo Jackson. Cecil Fielder had DHed for the Jays in the past, and Jose Canseco would be doing more of it for the Texas Rangers in the future.

On the other hand, salary caps and profit sharing might be the only approaches that would begin to even out the differences between the haves and have-nots. If something didn't change, there would be major and minor league teams in the majors, with teams like the Brewers and the Padres perpetually out of the running, with teams that only drank champagne and teams that never did. No other career had as yet demonstrated, as Paul Molitor's had, how much the disparity was affecting the sport.

There were two years left on his contract with the Blue Jays, plus an option year that would run past his 40th birthday. There could be several more seasons ahead, and they could be seasons spent on a team that would at least remain in contention. Moments hadn't passed before fans and reporters were already talking about the possibility of a "Three-peat" — a third consecutive World Series win for the Jays. But if they were looking for a legendary achievement, there was no reason to look to the future.

The '93 World Series had been a triumph for Blue Jays-style baseball. If predictions near the end of the season had proved true, the Atlanta Braves, with the best starting rotation in baseball, would have finally won the series. Instead, they weren't even there, beaten by the Phillies' incredibly disciplined hitting. The Jays had key pitching when it was most needed — Leiter in game one, Hentgen in game three, and Duane Ward too often to count — but their offense had made the difference, setting series records for runs and sacrifice flies.

One could measure the season and the World Series in statistics and awards, in personal marks and team victories, or one could talk about the things that Molitor had achieved that hadn't been done before by a player of his age or a player at his position. But the whole was greater than the sum of its parts. He was being welcomed into the pantheon of baseball. "I watch him and I say to myself 'there is probably the best hitter in the game today,'" observed the legendary Ted Williams. "He's the closest thing to Joe DiMaggio in the last 30 years. Matter of fact, every time I watch him I say 'there's Joe.'"

Molitor ended the 1993 post-season in the mythic time of baseball, scoring the winning run on Carter's series-ending homer, a feat which had occurred only once before, when Molitor was four years old, before the majority of the players on the field were born. Victory redeems the downtime and the rehab and the struggles of a career. He had lived for a while in the time of legend, when the work of a lifetime is focused in a magical instant and the team is joined in the special triumph of collective purpose.

Kristen Babb-Sprague and Linda Molitor (right).

P. POWER, THE TORONTO STAR

A World Series is much more than a sporting event — it's an opportunity for a city to see itself reflected in the eyes of the media. The character of a team is far more important when it makes its way to the World Series than during the regular season. No city could ever rouse the energy to attack the city of every team that comes to visit. It is a rivalry saved for the finals, when two cities already sufficiently pleased with being there come to develop a new sense of their own significance.

In the past two seasons, this has taken on special significance for Toronto and for Canada as well, as a Canadian team has finally made it into the series. After the 1992 ALCS victory, Dave Winfield had said, "We're keenly aware that we don't represent just a city. We represent an entire country. Every team has its territory of course, maybe a state or a region. But we've got all of Canada."

The attitude of other cities to the Jays is always a mystery to Toronto fans, just as the rest of Canada's attitudes to their city is a persistent mystery. Toronto is used to being hated by the rest of Canada, but the Blue Jays are treated as a national institution. When the Jays play in Seattle, fans come down from Vancouver to see them. When the Jays play in Milwaukee, they have fans from Northern Ontario and the prairies. Maritimers travel to Boston. It is almost as if the Giants and the Dodgers had kept their fans when they crossed America from New York to California.

Toronto fans are insistently loyal patrons. Some of the team's success must be directly credited to those who passed through the turnstiles at the old Exhibition Stadium and more recently at SkyDome in consistently record-breaking numbers. If the Jays are a wealthy team, it is that fan support that has made them wealthy. In the banner year of 1993, Philadelphia attendance passed the three-million mark in a stadium that seats 62,000. The Jays consistently draw four million fans to a stadium seating about 52,000. Were the Jays given the additional seating, there is no reason not to think they could draw five million fans a year during the regular season.

Toronto fans do not necessarily expect to win. Their hockey franchise was an embarrassment through much of the '70s and all of the '80s, until a change of ownership restored respectability in the '92–'93 season. The fans never deserted the team. That was why it was so bad. There was no incentive for the owners to provide a better product as long as they could sell out Maple Leaf Gardens. While the Jays had the reputation for choking, there was no adverse reaction at the turnstiles.

If Canadians have a national inferiority complex in relation to the United States, then the Blue Jays are part of that complicated relationship. It need not seem problematic for a Jays fan that their team could often be the best in baseball after 1985, but only make it to the World Series for the first time in 1992. Blue Jay fans often display a kind of indifference that is at the heart of their appreciation of the game. The exterior of SkyDome is festooned with sculptures of rowdy fans bursting out of their boxes. Yes, in Toronto there are statues of rowdy fans, but they have been at times the only rowdy fans the city possesses.

The Blue Jays are part of Canadian corporate culture, a culture that defines the city of Toronto. SkyDome, their state-of-the-art stadium, hulks beside the CN Tower, the tallest freestanding structure in the world, named for its owner, the state-owned railroad. Toronto has long struggled, like Chicago, with the idea of being "world class," but the city's campaign for recognition reveals Torontonians' belief that civic pride must be bestowed from without. In recent years the city has lost out on bids for both the Summer Olympics and the World's Fair. Montreal, long Toronto's chief Canadian rival, has had both. The 1992 World Series win by the Blue Jays was symbolic of more than baseball supremacy for the city. In Toronto, the word "world" has a special magnetism.

The expansion of major league baseball into Canada created a unique situation. The Montreal Expos were the first, in 1969, and the Blue Jays followed in 1977, but since the presence of one in the National League and the other in the American prevents them from meeting during the regular season, there isn't the rivalry one might expect. The Expos haven't advanced to post-season play since the NL championship of 1981, when the Jays finished their fifth season in last place.

The Jays have become very much a national team, a source of national pride, and because it's essentially American, the "World Series" is even more important. In part, it is redress for a national grievance.

Canadians love to dwell on American ignorance of Canadian geography and all things Canadian. In 1992, during a World Series game in Atlanta, a Marine honor guard carried the Canadian flag upside down. During the 1993 ALCS, the *Toronto Sun* published a column noting that Chicagoans couldn't find Toronto on the map. Many seemed to think it was on Lake Superior. Canadians always like to draw attention to such ignorance because in some sense it demonstrates their superiority to Americans: Canadians know so much, especially about them; they know so little, especially about Canadians. But there is a nagging undercurrent to the self-congratulation: the thought that Americans know so little because Canadians matter so little. The Blue Jays are a symbolic response to this neglect. There is a reason why so many comedians who target America — Dan Ackroyd, Martin Short, Mike Myers — are in fact Canadians.

It hardly matters that the Blue Jays are so many mercenaries, mostly continental Americans with a sprinkling of Puerto Ricans (an American protectorate) and citizens of the Domini-

TRACEY SAVEIN

can Republic (half an island so completely within the American thrall that it was once invaded by the United States with little protest). Only Rob Butler, an occasional fill-in, is a Canadian citizen. But the Jays are the expression of something else, of Canadian corporate know-how.

While the Americans have managed a free trade agreement that sees Canada regularly exporting jobs, raw materials, and whole industries, Canada has had a symbolic triumph in importing the cream of American baseball players to act as their representatives. In some respects the Blue Jays are a triumph of marketing. Their success at the box office has allowed them to bid on expensive free agents who have provided much of the team's excitement. Above all, they've exploited free agency to develop the identity and the quality of the product.

When teams make trades, they like to send their former workers as far away as possible: outside the division, outside the league, if the situation permits. It diminishes the chances of being embarrassed by the one they've given away. When the Jays traded young slugger Fred McGriff and Gold Glove shortstop Tony Fernandez, they sent them as far as they could: to San Diego, in exchange for Joe Carter and Roberto Alomar. San Diego was conscious of the distance as well. If there would be future embarrassment, that embarrassment would be as far away and as long away as possible. If fans met them again as opponents in a World Series, well, they couldn't complain too much.

But the Jays used free agency very differently and very pointedly. In the 1991 ALCS the Jays were defeated by the Minnesota Twins, who went on to win the World Series. Minnesota pitcher Jack Morris was series MVP. In the off-season, the Jays' most conspicuous foe entered free agency. Morris became a Blue Jay and managed to win a club record 21 games. In the 1992 season the stiffest competition in the AL East was offered by the Milwaukee Brewers. In one late-

August game, the Brewers defeated the Jays 22–2. In the off-season their most gifted hitter, Paul Molitor, elected for free agency. He became a Blue Jay. In the fifth game of the ALCS in 1992, Oakland's Dave Stewart pitched a complete-game win against the Blue Jays. In the off-season, Stewart too became a Blue Jay. In the middle of the 1993 season, when the A's were going nowhere and were willing to release Rickey Henderson for a million dollars for the months remaining on his expensive contract, the Jays acquired a player who had frequently embarrassed their pitchers in post-season play.

This is more than just exploiting free agency to stock an expensive team with talented veterans. As important as their skills are, these men already belong to the history of the team, its drama and its box office. Each player, already well known to Toronto fans, was an immediate addition to the team's image. Acquiring free agents is a way of capitalizing on team history to build an ever more exciting product. It's a way of snatching future victory from past defeat, or, in some cases, managing to win twice.

Yes, Dave Winfield killed a seagull and was led from the field by Toronto police to a chorus of boos, but now he has been a Blue Jay and he has finally taught Jays fans to cheer. Yes, Jack Morris beat the Jays, but now he's theirs. Yes, Dave Stewart beat them, but now he and his intimidating glare are theirs too. If Toronto could ultimately defeat Oakland when they had Stewart, how much surer the chances with him pitching for Toronto. Yes, Molitor chased the Jays in '87 and '92 and scored the first run in SkyDome, but now Toronto is his home. Yes, Rickey Henderson is an outrageous "hot dog" who has disconcerted and humiliated Toronto's pitching staff, but now Toronto fans cherish every slap catch, every long lead off first, every stolen base, every swaggering home run (there may not be many, but they belong to the Jays).

Even more important, the free agents have made the Jays

hungry and kept them hungry. By the late '80s the Jays had developed a reputation for choking, for being perhaps the most talented team in baseball but lacking the drive or unity to have that talent translate into post-season victory. The Blue Jays acquired character not through time but through trades and free agency. The Jays' key veterans in '92 — Winfield, Morris, Carter, and White — and in '93 — Stewart, Molitor, Carter, and White — were other people's veterans. The club's perennial lack of character was what permitted Beeston and Gillick to be as daring as they were. At the end of the '92 season they weren't just trying to save money. They didn't. They were trying to build another team with enough desire to win again. They did. After the '92 series, the vestiges of the Jays of the '80s — Stieb, Key, and Gruber — were gone. The younger stars of the Jays — Olerud, Alomar, Guzman, Hentgen — now belong to a tradition of winning.

There's a certain element of pathos in this, of course. Toronto has found ways to buy character, but as yet the organization hasn't been able to nurture a talent like Paul Molitor's or Dave Stewart's. It may be that such character has a hard time developing in the particular spotlight of Toronto baseball. As it does develop — in Alomar, Olerud, and Guzman — it will be, one way or another, somehow disconnected. Minneapolis-St. Paul, birthplace of Morris, Winfield, and Molitor, is the Toronto Blue Jays' symbolic northern wellspring.

In a sense, the Blue Jays' management have permitted Torontonians, and Canadians at large, something they seldom get in their exploited, self-effacing, and well-meaning lives: the sweet taste of revenge.

As the national team of Canada, the Jays have come to play an increasingly prominent role in political image-making. Long resented as the banking and corporate center by the rest of the country, Toronto is now emerging as something else — the home of the Blue Jays. People from the country's far-flung reaches make pilgrimages to SkyDome, where they unfurl banners declaring their hometowns in Newfoundland, Nova Scotia, Northern Ontario, and Manitoba to the national viewing audience. The Blue Jays are larger than Toronto.

During the 1992 national referendum on the Canadian constitution, then prime minister Brian Mulroney began to behave as if the survival of national interests depended simultaneously on voting "Yes" to his constitutional package and on the Blue Jays winning the World Series. With extraordinary twists of logic, the most enthusiastic of the media seemed to give the impression that if you didn't support the referendum, you were somehow letting the team down.

The '93 run to repeat as World Series champions was conducted at the same time as a national election. Anyone watching the news or reading the papers would imagine that the future of the country depended far more on the outcome of a series of baseball games than on the election. It became more and more apparent as the two campaigns progressed that people far preferred baseball players to politicians. The premier of New Brunswick, Frank McKenna, while defending Liberal leader Jean Chrétien against charges that he was too old to be an effective leader, cited Chrétien's vast experience . . . and compared him to Paul Molitor.

There was a reason for all this, apart from a general preference for athletes over politicians. When the Jays went to the World Series, Canada counted in the world in a way that it never seemed to count in politics. Winning the World Series could be a symbolic victory, while the North American Free Trade Agreement might be a long-term defeat. Free agency was a game Canada could win, and nobody embodied that game better than Paul Molitor.

The victory parade.
TRACEY SAVEIN

PAUL MOLITOR: TORONTONIAN
AND HONORARY CANADIAN

By the end of the World Series, Paul Molitor had, in seven months, become one of the most popular athletes in Toronto history. You could read it in the city's three daily newspapers, newspapers so different that they didn't usually even agree on what was news. The *Globe and Mail*, the most refined newspaper in Canada and one usually given to setting the standard in political, business, and cultural news, had gone so far as to publish a front-page list of the 15 things that made Molitor so popular. Two days later, the *Globe* was publishing a debate about the attractiveness of his butt. To the middlebrow *Toronto Star*, he was "Mr. Baseball," the winner of an informal "MVP" award before the season ended. To the tabloid *Toronto Sun* he was, well, just about everything. During the playoffs Molitor was given a byline, producing a short daily column in which he responded to an interviewer's questions about the team. For the Jays' victory parade, with Molitor in the lead car, he was provided with a camera so he could supply photographs of the happy throng from his perspective. It was an inspired idea. Torontonians were now "Torontonians as seen by Paul Molitor."

By the second game of the series, a banner had appeared in the SkyDome reading "Molitor for Prime Minister." By game six, on October 23, two days before the national election, there was another banner: "On October 25, Vote for Paul Molitor." They were signs that could only appear in Canada. Imagine a banner at a Pittsburgh Penguins game proclaiming, "Mario Lemieux for President." It wouldn't be flattering or insulting — it would be meaningless. President of what? The organization? The Players Association? "Molitor for Prime Minister," however, was less a joke than wishful thinking. He was articulate, modest, hardworking, disciplined, and forthright. It would be no contest.

Rob Butler, Danny Cox, Duane Ward, and
Paul Molitor during the SkyDome celebration.
TRACEY SAVEIN

Molitor's personality and presence fed the electoral fantasy. At the SkyDome reception the day after the victory, the highly unpopular premier of Ontario, Bob Rae, carried a placard promising he wouldn't make a speech. Molitor's own comments were almost a civics lesson: his expression of shared happiness extended from the team to the "city, province, and country." The city and the country's fondness for him knew no bounds of national origin. By year's end he was receiving votes as Canada's "Man of the Year."

Just as Molitor's reserve and modesty had always seemed special in the midwestern states where he'd spent his life and career, they took on special meaning for Canadians. Molitor asked the *Star*'s Rosie DiManno, "Where did you people learn to be so polite?" But, of course, Molitor was being polite to ask. DiManno thought he was more like a hockey player than a ballplayer: co-operative, hardworking, polite. That is, she thought he was like a Canadian.

Kirk Makin's front-page list in the *Globe and Mail* pinpointed 15 ways in which Molitor's reserve and hardwork made him unique. Touching on the talent, Makin called Molitor "a streak hitter — 162 games a year," though Molitor had never quite played in that many games in any regular season. Molitor didn't "embarrass God by publicly thanking Him after every RBI," which is a particular accomplishment considering Molitor's religious devotion. He didn't spit conspicuously or rearrange his crotch. He "actually means it when he says the team comes first," and unlike the loathed Kelly Gruber, Molitor "has never proclaimed himself the clubhouse leader." In the very year that he'd switched to Toronto, he was, according to Makin, "a traditionalist who'd happily play for one team forever." Makin was particularly impressed with the way Molitor's quiet intelligence affected the way he handled interviews. Molitor offered "fewer sports clichés in a year than most other athletes do in a sentence," and he seemed "aware

D. LOEK, THE TORONTO STAR

Doing charity work after the World Series.
JEFF GOODE, THE TORONTO STAR

there is no correlation between contract size and IQ."

In the days of the World Series and the weeks following, Molitor's commitment to Toronto became more and more evident. A few days after the series, when teammates had already departed for warmer climates and friendlier tax laws, Molitor was taking time to talk to terminal hospital patients by phone.

Molitor was the first Blue Jay star to make his residence in the city since the departure of Kelly Gruber, but some reporters were so unwilling to make that unpleasant connection that, by December 1993, he was being described by *Baseball Weekly* as the first Blue Jay to reside in the city since Rick Bosetti in 1980. It was a surprise for Canadians, who might grow accustomed to having the World Series trophy in Canada, but certainly didn't expect players in residence. In his usual modest way, Molitor said it was easier for him to move to Toronto than for other players, since he was used to the weather in Wisconsin and Minnesota. He was, however, the first in the troika of Minneapolis-St. Paul stars to make the move.

Moving was a sign of Molitor's commitment, both to his family and the city. From 1982 to 1987, Paul and Linda and later Blaire Molitor had spent the winters in warmer California, but after the year of the streak, the Molitors established permanent residence in Milwaukee. Molitor was concerned to keep the family together and provide a stable environment of friends and school for his growing daughter.

Moving to Toronto was also a way of giving something back to the city, as if more were needed, something that he had always done in Minneapolis-St. Paul and Milwaukee, where he was as well liked for his commitment to his community as he was for his accomplishments on the field. In Toronto, Molitor was already on the advisory board of the Clarke Institute's Call for Courage campaign, involving rehabilitation for people recovering from mental or physical injuries. He also participated in the team's Hit the Books campaign in local schools and continued to be very active in the Make a Wish Foundation. He and Linda had walked in a march for AIDS awareness, and they maintained their involvement in fighting childhood cancer.

In Toronto, where baseball stars have always been an exotic species, Molitor's involvement could come to mean even more than it had in Milwaukee. There was something very special about having a World Series MVP, a potential Hall of Fame player, in Toronto. It gave a humane face to the game, just as Dave Stewart had when he delayed his trip to Chicago in the middle of the ALCS to stay in Toronto to help feed the homeless during Canadian Thanksgiving. Stewart, for his part, was surprised when Pat Gillick had shown up at the shelter. He had never seen a team executive during similar projects in Oakland. Later, Stewart returned to Toronto at Christmas to do the same with more turkey dinners. In seeking free agents after the first series win, Paul Beeston and Pat Gillick had probably chosen the best ambassadors the sport could have.

Molitor's popularity was compounded of the way he played the game, the way he carried himself on the field and off, and the way he linked the city and the game. It's apparent in the kinds of things that DiManno and Makin found exceptional. He bridged the gap between the city and its ball players in new ways.

People often comment on the way major league sports are like war games or tribal competitions, in which teams of hired professionals somehow represent the city's courage and skill. While the analogy may be true, it is also the case that on each side there are already two tribes, the team and the city. The gap between team and city is widest in a place like Toronto, which lacks a strong indigenous tradition of the game. The members of the team are joined by the culture and the history

*Joking with David Letterman, while
the Phillies Lenny Dykstra looks on.*

AP PHOTO

of the sport itself, and by the caste of professionals who often move from team to team. Their interest in team success is direct, reflected by continued and improved employment. The city, for its part, often finds itself successful on the field in direct proportion to the extent to which it supports the team.

The way ball players behave on the field and the specific mannerisms of the profession are somehow essential to their identity. It is part of the culture of the game to spit and rearrange your genitals in a crowded stadium. It is almost a ritual of concentration. The player pays attention to the game, not how he might appear on television.

But it's more than that. The spitting and tugging are private acts conducted in public. They're a way of taking control, of diminishing the obtrusive audience. They're also part of the territorial imperative of baseball: "I spit and I scratch to possess this space." It's true, too, of batting stances. John Kruk, the Phillies first baseman, has a primitive genius for this stuff. In the batter's box, he stands perfectly erect, his hands raised to head level, twirling his bat over his head as if the object of the game might be to see how far you can throw the bat into the outfield. When talk-show host David Letterman asked Molitor what it's like to arrive on first base with Kruk, Molitor replied, "Basically he tries to convince you, you were lucky to get a hit. And he spits on your shoes a lot." It's a very territorial game.

Molitor brings an utterly different personal style to the game. His batting stance is classically upright and utterly motionless. As a designated hitter, he's a man who has had to learn to live without a fielder's sense of, and needs for, the territorial. In notoriously reserved Canada, he doesn't appear to spit or rearrange his privates, or, perhaps even better, he does so discreetly. When he is running the bases, he is not concerned about possession of the base he is on. His territorial drive is always focused on the next base.

While he may have surrendered some of baseball's more conspicuous territorial urges, Molitor has come in a single season to possess Toronto as no player before him has. It is almost as if he has taken the time to understand the city. He is an urban ball player, and an urbane one as well. When he claims the Blue Jays have more cellular phones, that they're "genteel," he's not just being witty. He's defining the culture of the city itself, its self-absorption, its sophistication, even its ironic awareness of its own materialism. If Toronto could choose the perfect player to represent it, it would be Molitor. And, by luck, it has him.

When Molitor decided to move to Toronto, he wasn't just moving. For Toronto, he was uniting the two tribes of baseball in the city, bringing the team and the city together in a way they had never been together before. For Toronto, shell-shocked by economic downturn, Paul Molitor embodies qualities it would like to possess. Civilized and yet still sincere, he is also a survivor, a man who has endured time in the hinterlands, who works harder in times of adversity, and who is humble in triumph.

PAUL MOLITOR'S MAJOR
LEAGUE BATTING STATISTICS

YR	BA	G	AB	R	H	2B	3B	HR	RBI	SB
78	.273	125	521	73	142	26	4	6	45	30
79	.322	140	584	88	188	27	16	9	62	33
80	.304	111	450	81	137	29	2	9	37	34
81	.267	64	251	45	67	11	0	2	19	10
82	.302	160	666	136	201	26	8	19	71	41
83	.270	152	608	95	164	28	6	15	47	41
84	.217	13	46	3	10	1	0	0	6	1
85	.297	140	576	93	171	28	3	10	48	21
86	.281	105	437	62	123	24	6	9	55	20
87	.353	118	465	114	164	41	5	16	75	45
88	.312	154	609	115	190	34	6	13	60	41
89	.315	155	615	84	194	35	4	11	56	27
90	.285	103	418	64	119	27	6	12	45	18
91	.325	158	665	133	216	32	13	17	75	19
92	.320	158	609	89	195	36	7	12	89	31
93	.332	160	636	121	211	37	5	22	111	22
LIFE	.306	2016	8156	1396	2492	442	91	182	901	434

WORKS CONSULTED

The following abbreviations have been used for frequent sources: *GM* for *Globe and Mail*; *MJ* for *Milwaukee Journal*; *MS* for *Milwaukee Sentinel*; *Star* for *Toronto Star*; *Sun* for *Toronto Sun*. Descriptions are as accurate as possible, but in the case of some sources, page numbers were not readily available.

Albert, J.L. "Getting Better All the Time." *USA Today* 25 Oct. 1993: 7C.

"American League Notes." *Baseball Weekly* 15–28 Dec. 1993: 11.

"Angels Proving Strength on Mound, Jackson Says." *Star* 8 Oct. 1982: B2.

Another World: The Toronto Star's Tribute to the '93 Blue Jays. Toronto: Doubleday, 1993.

Antonen, Mel. "Molitor Lives Dream and Is Named MVP." *USA Today* 25 Oct. 1993: 7C.

"AP Makes Molitor an All-Star Choice." *MJ* 29 Oct. 1987: 1C, 4C.

Aschburner, Steve. "Yount MVP for All Seasons." *MJ* 18 Oct. 1982.

Bauman, Michael. "Molitor Living in Land of Greats." *MJ* 21 Aug. 1987: 1A, 7A.

——— . "Molitor Now Looks Cool in Brewers' Hot Corner." *MJ* 1 May 1983.

"Baylor Powers Angels to Win." *Star* 6 Oct. 1982: D1.

Bengtson, Tom. "Former Gopher 'Superstar' Shines Brightly as a Brewer." *Minneapolis Daily* 19 Oct. 1982.

Berghaus, Bob. "Bando Returns Home as Mr. Unpopular." *MJ* 10 Dec. 1992: 1, 5.

——— . "Final Seconds Clicking Down on Molitor Era." *MJ* 7 Dec. 1992: C1, C2.

——— . "Red Sox Show Interest in Molitor." *MJ* 6 Dec. 1992: C1, C10.

Bishop, Morin. "More Than Halfway There." *Sports Illustrated* 24 Aug. 1987: 26–27.

Blatchford, Christie. "Stew-pendous." *Sun* 13 Oct. 1993: 5.

"Bonds Earns Top Spot, but Four Jays Ranked among Baseball's Best Players." *Star* 28 Oct. 1993: C1.

Boswell, Thomas. "Molitor Deserves the Spotlight." *MJ* 20 Aug. 1987.

Braun, Rick. "Deer: Greatest Day of My Life." *MS* 20 Apr. 1987: 1, 5.

"Brewers, Braves Clinch Titles." *Star* 4 Oct. 1982.

"Brewers Pick a Big Ten Star." *MS* 11 June 1977.

Brunt, Stephen. "It's Just the Way the Phillies Are." *GM* 16 Oct. 1993: A1, A8.

——— . "Molitor Family Finds Toronto Quite Neighbourly." *GM* 12 Apr. 1993: D5.

Buffery, Steve. "Even a Phillie Loves Molly." *Sun* 20 Oct. 1993: 66.

——— . "Molitor Was Inspiration." *Sun* 13 Oct. 1993: 72.

——— . "Phillies Watch." *Sun* 24 Oct. 1993.

Burke, Don. "In His Last At-Bat, Molitor Delivers." *MJ* 14 Aug. 1987: 1C, 4C.

——— . "It's 37 and Counting." *MJ* 23 Aug. 1987: 1C, 7C.

——— . "Men of Steal Lead Brewers." *MJ* 27 July 1987.

——— . "Molitor Believes Vets Have Key Roles." *MJ* 21 Apr. 1987.

——— . "Molitor, Gantner May Switch Positions." *MJ* 10 Nov. 1987: 1C, 2C.

——— . "Molitor Gets No Style Points, but Extends Streak to 29 Games." *MJ* 15 Aug. 1987.

——— . "Molitor Is Becoming a National Topic." *MJ* 19 Aug. 1987.

——— . "Scoop on a Streak." *MJ* 24 Aug. 1987.

——— . "Up to 35, It's a Streak That's Fit to Be Tied." *MJ* 21 Aug. 1987: 1C, 2C.

Campbell, Neil A. "Gaston's Thinking about Winning One for Molitor." *GM* 23 Oct. 1993: A30.

——— . "Jays Pour It On to Storm Past Phillies." *GM* 20 Oct. 1993.

——— . "Jays Wise to Frowsy Phils." *GM* 16 Oct. 1993: A18.

——— . "Molitor's Cocaine Problem Chronicled." *GM* 29 Sept. 1993: C8.

——— . "Molitor Set to Prove Himself." *GM* 24 Feb. 1993: C6.

——— . "Odds Favour Quick Ending to Title Hunt." *GM* 27 Sept. 1993: D1.

——— . "Small Cities Can't Compete for Players, Ex-Brewer Says." *GM* 20 Jan. 1993: C8.

—— . "Teammates Value Molitor's Efforts." *GM* 16 Sept. 1993: E7.

—— . "Timlin Ruins Molitor's Night in Milwaukee." *GM* 26 June 1993: A20.

Chapman, Lou. "Augie, Molitor Keep Ship Afloat." *MS* 21 Sept. 1978.

—— . "Molitor's Hit Turns Jays Blue." *MS* 17 Aug. 1978.

—— . "Molitor Star as Brewers Gain Split." *MS* 19 June 1978.

—— . "Pact Puts Molitor in Groove." *MS* 13 Mar. 1979.

—— . "Two Brewer 'Unknowns' Pace Victory." *MS* 3 Aug. 1979.

"Charity the Blue Jay Way." *Sun* 13 Oct. 1993: 3.

Chass, Murray. "Molitor Gets to See Another Side of the Chase." *New York Times* 25 Oct. 1993: B5, B7.

"Chitown Thinks We're 'Superior.'" *Sun* 6 Oct. 1993: 3.

Christl, Cliff. "Bittersweet 'Revenge.'" *MJ* 31 Mar. 1989: 1C, 4C.

—— . "Brewers Starting Their Own $3 Million Club." *MJ* 21 Feb. 1990.

—— . "Dalton's Long Fall from Grace." *MJ* 6 Oct. 1991: C1, C8.

—— . "Molitor Swings to Help the Team." *MJ* 15 June 1990.

—— . "Molitor Unable to Play after Injuring Finger." *MJ* 18 June 1990.

Cohen, Jim. "The Other Gorman." *MJ* 24 Aug. 1983.

Curry, Jack. "Molitor, a Blue Jay with Big Red Eyes." *New York Times* 25 Oct. 1993: B7.

DiManno, Rosie. *Glory Jays: Canada's World Series Champions*. Champaign, IL: Sagamore, 1993.

—— . "Jays Run 1–2–3 in Batting Race." *Star* 4 Oct. 1993: B1, B7.

—— . "Molitor Prepares for Turn in Field." *Star* 15 Oct. 1993: C2.

—— . "Molly-Ball Wins for Jays." *Star* 20 Oct. 1993: A1, A4.

—— . "Paul Molitor: Mr. Baseball." *Star* 5 Oct. 1993: B4.

—— . "Two in a Row on Joltin' Joe's Big Home Run." *Star* 24 Oct. 1993: A1, A16.

Dodd, Mike. "Gaston Plays Victory Low Key; Players Say He's Key to Success." *USA Today* 25 Oct. 1993: 7C.

Dougherty, Mike. "All Eyes on Molitor as Streak Reaches 36." *MJ* 22 Aug. 1987: 9A, 10A.

Elliott, Bob. "Hisle Out as Jays Coach." *Sun* 22 Oct. 1993: B6.

—— . "Stewart Shows His Heart." *Sun* 13 Oct. 1993: 67.

—— . "Take the Money and Run." *Sun* 12 Feb. 1994: SP17.

—— . "U. of Minnesota Cashes In." *Sun* 21 Oct. 1993: 77.

Feuerherd, Vic. "Angels Grab 2–0 Series Lead." *MS* 7 Oct. 1982.

—— . "Brewers Dominate AL Offensive Statistics." *MS* 5 Oct. 1982.

——— . "Molitor Happy with First Brewer Offer." *MS* 31 Dec. 1982.

——— . "Molitor Hurt in 4–3 Victory." *MS* 4 May 1981.

——— . "Molitor's Slam Rips Blue Jays." *MS* 23 Apr. 1981.

——— . "Molitor's 3 Homers Can't Save Brewers." *MS* 13 May 1982.

——— . "Sox Bomb Brewers with 20 Hits." *MS* 14 May 1982.

Fidlin, Ken. "Molitor Makes Cito Look Great." *Sun* 20 Oct. 1993: 63.

Flaherty, Tom. "Barker Masters Brewers." *MJ* 13 Aug. 1981.

——— . "Brewers' Bubble Hasn't Burst." *MJ* 15 Apr. 1987.

——— . "Brewers Give Bambi an Ungrand Finale." *MJ* 8 Sept. 1986.

——— . "Brewers Ride Molitor's Streak." *MJ* 10 Aug. 1987: 1C, 4C.

——— . "Current Brew Crew Cut Above the Past." *MJ* 19 June 1978.

——— . "Fans Issue Mandate for Molitor at 2nd." *MJ* 7 July 1988.

——— . "Fifth Time Is a Charm for Molitor." *MJ* 22 July 1983.

——— . "Good Health Will Be a Bonus for Brewers' Molitor." *MJ* 7 Jan. 1988.

——— . "Injury-Prone Molitor Out with a Groin Pull." *MJ* 3 June 1987.

——— . "It's Official: Molitor's at 2nd." *MJ* 14 Mar. 1988: 1C.

——— . "It's True! Brewers in 1st." *MJ* 12 July 1982.

——— . "Manning Stars, Thanks to Molitor." *MJ* 31 May 1986.

——— . "Molitor Back with 2 Hits; Brewers Edge Tribe Again." *MJ* 28 Aug. 1987: 1.

——— . "Molitor Better, but Will Wait." *MJ* 7 July 1987: 1C.

——— . "Molitor Declines Arbitration Offer." *MJ* 19 Dec. 1987.

——— . "Molitor Extends His Streak to 23 Games." *MJ* 9 Aug. 1987.

——— . "Molitor, Molitor, Molitor." *MJ* 20 Aug. 1986.

——— . "Molitor Overcomes Ankle Injury." *MJ* 10 Aug. 1987: 1C.

——— . "Molitor Power Knocks Sox Off." *MJ* 11 Aug. 1988.

——— . "Molitor's Contract to Pay $5 Million." *MJ* 17 Feb. 1983.

——— . "Molitor Signs with Brewers for 5 Years." *MJ* 16 Feb. 1983.

——— . "Molitor Survives Injury, Brush with Drugs." *MJ* 15 Aug. 1985: 1, 2.

——— . "Molitor Wants to Stay Awhile." *MJ* 17 Dec. 1987.

——— . "Most Brewers Agree with Ueberroth's Plan." *MJ* 2 Mar. 1986.

——— . "Moving On: For Molitor, Leaving Isn't Easy." *MJ* 9 Dec. 1992: C1, C3.

——— . "Playing in Japan Was Fun for Molitor." *MJ* 16 Nov. 1988.

——— . "Power Show No Big Help to Brewers." *MJ* 13 May 1982.

——— . "Truly Blue Crew: Sad End to Molitor Era." *MJ* 8 Dec. 1992: C3.

Gano, Rick. "Molitor Says Farewell." *GM* 9 Dec. 1993: C6.

Geracie, Bud. "Molitor Fears Broken Hand." *MS* 28 May 1983.

Getto, Dennis. "Part of the Winning Team: Brewers' Families Never Strike Out." *MJ* 11 Oct. 1982.

Gilbert, Craig. "Molitor Is FANtastic!" *MJ* 22 Aug. 1987: 1A, 20A.

Gohring, Mike. "Sizzling Brewers Double Boil Blue Jays." *MJ* 17 Aug. 1978.

Gordon, Alison. "Brewers Back from Brink." *Star* 10 Oct. 1981: D1.

——— . "Brewers Came Away Empty in the Last Game That Mattered." *Star* 21 Oct. 1982: D2.

——— . "Wisconsin Fans Egg On Brewers." *Star* 17 Oct. 1982: E2.

——— . "Yankees' Power Booms Again." *Star* 11 Oct. 1981: B1.

Greenberg, Jay. "Happy Mother's Day, Cito." *Sun* 20 Oct. 1993: 65.

——— . "The Last Word." *Sun* 26 Oct. 1993: 70.

——— . "Father Paul Knows Best." *Sun* 25 Oct. 1993: 52.

——— . "Straight Talk Solved the Problem." *Sun* 21 Oct. 1993: 72.

Harrington, Kevin. "Great Big Hug: Fans Greet Brewers." *MJ* 5 Oct. 1992: 1, 5.

Hart, Mike. "Fans Given What They Came For." *MS* 22 Aug. 1987.

——— . "Molitor Says Players Back Union's Stand." *MS* 16 July 1985.

——— . "Plesac Pulls Out Brewers' Victory." *MS* 17 July 1987.

Haudricourt, Tom. "Big Pact Sought for Molly." *MS* 18 Nov. 1987: 1, 2.

——— . "Brewers Crash Toronto Party." *MS* 6 June 1989.

——— . "Brewers Get Caught Up with Streak." *MS* 19 Aug. 1987: 1, 2.

——— . "Brewers Overjoyed Molitor Bringing His Streak Home." *MS* 21 Aug. 1987: 1A, 18.

——— . "Brewers Show Poise in Media Spotlight." *MS* 21 Apr. 1987: 1, 2.

——— . "Brewers Tip Tribe in Slugfest 11–7." *MS* 31 May 1986.

——— . "Brewers Use Bunts to Ground Jays." *MS* 9 Sept. 1987.

——— . "Brock to Seek Trade If Molitor Plays 1st Base." *MS* 28 July 1990: 1, 2.

——— . "Keltner's Eye on Molitor's Hitting Streak." *MS* 20 Aug. 1987.

——— . "Knudson, Brewers Handle Tribe." *MS* 18 Aug. 1987: 1, 2.

——— . "Major Overhaul of Roster Leaves Brewers Optimistic." *MS* Feb. 1987.

——— . "Molitor Activated: Mirabella Demoted." *MS* 26 May 1987: 1, 3.

——— . "Molitor Becomes a Blue Jay." *MS* 8 Dec. 1992: 1A, 11A.

——— . "Molitor Earning His Incentive Pay." *MS* 16 Sept. 1988: 1, 2.

——— . "Molitor Explains Request." *MS* 25 Jan. 1990: 1, 4.

——— . "Molitor Files for Free Agency." *MS* 30 Oct. 1987: 1.

——— . "Molitor Gets $9.1 Million, Waives Free Agency." *MS* 20 Feb. 1990: 1, 2.

——— . "Molitor Has Dream Game." *MS* 20 Aug. 1986.

——— . "Molitor Ignites Brewers' Victory." *MS* 20 Aug. 1987: 1, 2.

——— . "Molitor Leads the Way for Brewers." *MS* 29 July 1987.

——— . "Molitor Makes 3rd Comeback of '86 Season." *MS* 9 July 1986.

——— . "Molitor Might Reject Salary Arbitration." *MS* 17 Dec. 1987: 1, 2.

——— . "Molitor Out 3 Weeks with Finger Injury." *MS* 31 Mar. 1989: 1, 5.

——— . "Molitor, Pitchers Stay Hot." *MS* 22 Aug. 1987: 1, 2.

——— . "Molitor Placed on Disabled List." *MS* 12 May 1986: 1.

——— . "Molitor Placed on Disabled List." *MS* 19 June 1990: 1, 2.

——— . "Molitor Placed on DL, Could Be Out a Month." *MS* 3 Apr. 1990: 1, 2.

——— . "Molitor Says He Isn't Depressed." *MS* 28 Aug. 1987: 1, 11.

——— . "Molitor's Homer Not Enough." *MS* 14 Aug. 1987.

——— . "Molitor's Latest Injury Could Bring Changes." *MS* 28 Mar. 1988: 1, 5.

——— . "Molitor's Streak Ends." *MS* 27 Aug. 1987: 1, 10.

——— . "Molitor's Thefts Ignite Brewers." *MS* 27 July 1987.

——— . "Molitor Surgery Called a Success." *MS* 20 June 1990.

——— . "Molitor Voted Starting All-Star 2nd Baseman." *MS* 7 July 1988: 1, 2.

——— . "Molly Pact Is a Relief to Brewers." *MS* 7 Jan. 1988: 1.

——— . "Sveum Steals Spotlight with 2 HRs." *MS* 15 Aug. 1987.

——— . "Timing Leaves Molitor Cool." *MS* 29 Sept. 1993: 1B, 3B.

——— . "Treb Wants All Coaches Back in '91." *MS* 29 Sept. 1990: 1, 2.

"Hit Parade." *Sports Illustrated* 31 Aug. 1987: 13.

Hoffer, Richard. "Career Move." *Sports Illustrated* 29 Mar. 1993: 44–49.

Houston, William. "Truth & Rumours: The Be All and End All." *GM* 22 Oct. 1993: C13.

——— . "Truth and Rumours: Spit and Unpolished." *GM* 1 Nov. 1993: D4.

Hunt, Jim. "Anger Fuels Jays Trio." *Sun* 26 Oct. 1993: 52.

"It's a Sweep for Thomas." *Star* 11 Nov. 1993: C1.

Janz, William. "Holy Hit Streak!" *MS* 22 Aug. 1987: 1, 7.

Johnson, Chuck. "Hisle's Celebration Muted by Job Uncertainty." *USA Today* 25 Oct. 1993: 7C.

Kausler, Don. "Brewers Have the Worst Base-Stealing Record in Major Leagues." *MS* 19 May 1981.

———. "Martinez Stops Brewers, 1–0." *MS* 18 July 1980.

Kendall, Pete. "Molitor's an All-Star — But Will He Play?" *MJ* 1 July 1980.

Kenney, Ray. "Molitor Hasn't Exploited His On-Field Heroics." *MJ* 26 Nov. 1987.

The Late Show with David Letterman. CBS 26 Oct. 1993.

MacCarl, Neil. "Cards Singing in the Rain." *Star* 19 Oct. 1982.

———. "Series Win Was in Cards." *Star* 21 Oct. 1982: D1, D3.

———. "Spirit of St. Louis Dampened." *Star* 13 Oct. 1982.

———. "Yount Sparkles as Brewers Put Cards in Hole." *Star* 18 Oct. 1982: B2.

Makin, Kirk. "15 Ways Molitor Scores." *GM* 20 Oct. 1993: A1.

Malamud, Bernard. *The Natural.* New York: Farrar, 1952.

Mandel, Michele. "Molly's Living a Dream." *Sun* 24 Oct. 1993: 35.

Mariotti, Jay. "Sox Just Love Hatred." *Sun* 9 Oct. 1993: SP7.

Martino, Sam. "From One Who Knows: Molitor Warns of Drugs." *MJ* 2 June 1987: 1A, 8A.

McHale, Jack. "Paul Molitor Talks to Jack McHale." *GM* 14 June 1993: D2.

Millson, Larry. "Carter Tears Strip off Columnist." *GM* 22 Oct. 1993: C14.

———. "Gaston Mum on Molitor." *GM* 16 Oct. 1993: A18.

———. "It's Dollars and Sense as Jays Deal Gruber." *GM* 9 Dec. 1992: C8, C6.

———. "Jays Half Way to Victory." *GM* 20 Oct. 1993: A1.

———. "Molitor Displays His Manifold Talents." *GM* 17 May 1993: D4.

———. "Molitor Puts Cap on Brewer Past." *GM* 25 May 1993: C6.

———. "MVP at Peace amid the Din." *Star* 26 Oct. 1993: C3.

———. "Yount Continues His Assault on the Jays." *GM* 28 May 1993: D14.

Molitor, Paul. "Insider." *Sun* 6 Oct. 1993: 62.

———. "Insider." *Sun* 7 Oct. 1993: 70.

———. "Insider." *Sun* 22 Oct. 1993: 90.

———. "Insider: Aggression Will Defeat McDowell." *Sun* 10 Oct. 1993: 68.

———. "Insider: Anxiety Filled Up the Air." *Sun* 13 Oct. 1993: 69.

———. "Insider: Demands, Demands." *Sun* 16 Oct. 1993: J28.

———. "Insider: Devo Rates Praise." *Sun* 18 Oct. 1993: 53.

———. "Insider: Excited to Be In." *Sun* 21 Oct. 1993: 77.

———. "Insider: Henderson Production a Big Plus." *Sun* 11 Oct. 1993: 33.

———. "Insider: Jays Up to Challenge." *Sun* 12 Oct. 1993: 65.

———. "Insider: Mulholland Hangs Tough." *Sun* 23 Oct. 1993: SP8.

———. "Insider: Nerves No Factor." *Sun* 17 Oct. 1993: 81.

———. "Insider: Phillies Looking Familiar." *Sun* 8 Oct. 1993: 72.

———. "Insider: Research Explains Unknown." *Sun* 9 Oct. 1993: C9.

———. "Insider: Sorry to See Hisle Go." *Sun* 24 Oct. 1993: 73.

———. "Insider: Strange Feeling Over at Third." *Sun* 15 Oct. 1993: 84.

———. "Insider: Watching the Worst." *Sun* 20 Oct. 1993: 68.

———. "Insider: Win Slowly Sinking In." *Sun* 14 Oct. 1993: 78.

"Molitor an MVP to Boy with Leukemia." *Star* 27 Oct. 1993: E5.

"Molitor at 27." *MJ* 13 Aug. 1987.

"Molitor, Brewers Agree." *MJ* 5 Feb. 1981.

"Molitor Comes Back; Edwards Farmed Out." *MS* 13 Aug. 1981.

"Molitor Explains, Reflects on Signing with Toronto." *MJ* 8 Dec. 1992: C2.

"Molitor Gets Praise after Brewer Loss." *MS* 11 Mar. 1978.

"Molitor Joins Free Agent Game." *MJ* 30 Oct. 1987: C1, C2.

"Molitor Makes It 3 Straight." *MJ* 19 Aug. 1979.

"Molitor May Net 4 Million." *MS* 17 Feb. 1983.

"Molitor Returns to Infield." *MJ* 4 Sept. 1987.

"Molitor Runs Amok against Athletics." *GM* 27 July 1987: C4.

"Molitor Signs." *MS* 6 Feb. 1981.

"Molitor's Streak Gets New Twist." *MJ* 18 Aug. 1987.

"Molitor's 31 Straight Ties Him with Landreaux." *MJ* 17 Aug. 1987.

"Molitor to Get Service Award." *MS* 27 Oct. 1990.

"Molitor to Team: Ignore Drug Plan." *MJ* 25 Sept. 1985: 1, 2.

Morrison, Scott. *Back 2 Back: Toronto Blue Jays 1993 World Champions.* Toronto: Canada Wide Feature Service, 1993.

1993 Baseball Almanac. Lincolnwood, IL: Signet, 1993.

"1993 Blue Jay Records." *Star* 4 Oct. 1993: B1.

Olson, Andy. "When Brewers Talk, Kids Listen." *MJ* 19 May 1988.

O'Malley, Martin. "Cito Gaston: When Winning Is Not Enough." *GM* 16 Oct. 1993: A18, 17.

"Once Again Injury Bites Molitor." *MJ* 30 Apr. 1987: 1C, 4C.

Perkins, Dave. "AL Manager Award Should Have Cito's Name on It." *Star* 26 Oct. 1993: C1, C3.

——. "Jays Just Taking Care of Business." *Star* 24 Sept. 1993: E3.

——. "Jays Must Now Get Past Wrath of Baltimore Fans." *Star* 30 Sept. 1993: C3.

——. "Let's Not Forget Olerud in Post-Season Puffery." *Star* 4 Oct. 1993: B1, B10.

——. "Molitor's More Than Worth the Money for Jays." *Star* 16 Sept. 1993: D1, D6.

——. "New Rules No Problem for Blue Jay Juggernaut." *Star* 20 Oct. 1993: B2.

——. "Stewart Welcomes Game 6 Challenge." *Star* 12 Oct. 1993: E2.

——. "Stottlemyre Baffles Red Sox." *Star* 22 Sept. 1993: C1.

Rapoport, Ron. *The Los Angeles Daily News.* 24 Oct. 1993. Qtd. in "Just What Was Said." *GM* 25 Oct. 1993: D4.

"Report Molitor Pact $5 Million." *MS* 18 Feb. 1983.

Rohde, Marie. "Brewers Take Time Out for Prayer." *MJ* 23 May 1988.

Rushin, Steve. "It's Party Time." *Sports Illustrated* (Canadian edition) 1 Nov. 1993: 12–29.

Rutsey, Mike. "2-ronto the Great." *Sun* 24 Oct. 1993: 66.

——. "Jays Watch." *Sun* 24 Oct. 1993: 70.

——. "Lengthy Debate Ends with Molitor at First." *Sun* 20 Oct. 1993: 64.

Ryan, Allan. "Book Clouds Molitor's Celebration." *Star* 29 Sept. 1993: C1.

——. "Good Golly Molly!" *Star* 20 Oct. 1993: B1, B2.

——. " 'I Wasn't Bad' at Third Base, Molitor Says." *Star* 21 Oct. 1993: C3.

——. "Oh, Deer! Blue Jays Finally Lose." *Star* 23 Sept. 1993: C1.

——. "Sprague at Third for Now." *Star* 5 Oct. 1993: F5.

Sabljak, Mark. "Brewers to Salute Molitor and Fans." *MJ* 10 Sept. 1987.

Salituro, Chris. "Molitor and Yount Missing; So Is Brewers' Punch." *MJ* 15 June 1980: 11, 12.

Sauerberg, George. "Brewer Success Credited to 'Fearsome Foursome.' " *MS* 5 June 1980: 1, 3.

——. "Brewers Vote 33–0 to Strike." *MS* 29 Mar. 1980: 1, 3.

Schmitt, Mary. "Paulie among the Elite as 39-Game Streak Ends." *MJ* 27 Aug. 1987: 1, 2.

Scott, Terry. "Baseball Thrives in Spite of Itself." *GM* 23 Dec. 1993: C8.

Simmons, Steve. "The Last Word." *Sun* 20 Oct. 1993: 86.

——. "The Last Word." *Sun* 25 Oct. 1993: 82.

——. "Molitor Leading the Way." *Sun* 7 Oct. 1993: 68.

Slater, Tom. "Molitor Gives Way to Olerud Tonight." *Star* 20 Oct. 1993: B3.

Sugar, Bert Randolph, ed. *Baseballistics*. New York: St. Martin's, 1990.

"Sutton Saves the Day for Battling Brewers." *Star* 9 Oct. 1982.

"There Is No Joy in Milwaukee." *Star* 21 Oct. 1982: D2.

Vecsey, George. "Joe Carter Puts an End to the World Series." *New York Times* 25 Oct. 1993: A1, B7.

Verducci, Tom. "The Complete Player." *Sports Illustrated* (Canadian ed.) 1 Nov. 1993: 30–33.

Vieira, Paul, and Farhan Memon. "Jubilant Fans Party Peacefully in Jays' Honour." *GM* 25 Oct. 1993: A13.

Walters, Charley. "Angels High on Molitor." *St. Paul Dispatch* 21 June 1976.

White, Paul. "Fire Up the Grill, San Diego." *Baseball Weekly* 16 Nov. 1993: 2.

Williams, Dick, and Bill Plaschke. *No More Mr. Nice Guy*. San Diego: Harcourt, 1990.

Wolfley, Bob. "Closer to Home." *MJ* 11 Dec. 1992.

Wong, Gregg. "Brewers Draft U's Molitor on First Round." *St. Paul Pioneer Press* 8 June 1977.

Wong, Tony. "1 Million Jam Downtown to Revel in Jays' Big Win." *Star* 24 Oct. 1993: A2.

Woolsey, Garth. "Bell Might Get Call as DH in White Sox's New Order." *Star* 12 Oct. 1993: E2.

——. " 'Thankful' Molitor Savors MVP Moment." *Star* 24 Oct. 1993: D3.

"World Series Records Set or Tied in '93." *USA Today* 25 Oct. 1993: 7C.

York, Marty. "Molitor Plays Phone Games." *GM* 30 Sept. 1987: D2.

Zeisberger, Mike. " 'Cheap Shot' Irks Molitor." *Sun* 29 Sept. 1993: 69.

——. "Clinched!" *Sun* 28 Sept. 1993: 53.

——. "First and Foremost: Molitor Ignites Blue Jays Rout with Homer, Triple." *Sun* 20 Oct. 1993: 62.

——. " 'I don't know' on Third." *Sun* 16 Oct. 1993: J5.

——. "Ironic Win for Molitor." *Sun* 28 Sept. 1993: 55.

———. "Jays Watch." *Sun* 13 Oct. 1993: 67.

———. "Molitor Goes 3rd to 1st." *Sun* 18 Oct. 1993: 50.

———. "Molitor's Command Cito's Wish." *Sun* 21 Oct. 1993: 72.

———. "Mr. Perseverance." *Sun* 5 Oct. 1993: BJ12.